World Watch

The World Around Us

Themes	Unit	
Planet Earth	Landscapes	2
Rivers	A Wet Planet	8
Weather	Hot and Cold Places	14
Settlement	A Place to Live	20
Transport	Ways of Travelling	26
Work	Food and Farming	32
Environment	Caring for the Countryside	38

Places

United Kingdom	Scotland	44
Europe	France	50
World	Asia	56
	Glossary	62
	Index	63

Planet Earth

Landscapes

What is the earth's surface like?

Our world is one of nine planets that spin around the sun. We call it the earth.

From far out in space the earth looks quite small. You can see it is round like a ball.

The earth is a very special planet. There is just the right mix of rock, air and water for animals and plants to live. No other planet is quite the same.

Water covers most of the earth's surface. There are many different seas and oceans. The Pacific Ocean is the largest.

The land is divided into great blocks called continents. Some of the land is very flat. In other places there are mountains, forests and deserts.

The surface of the earth and the moon.

Fact file

- The earth takes a year to spin around the sun.
- There are seven continents. They are Europe, Asia, North America, South America, Africa, Australasia and Antarctica.

Talking and writing

1 Which of the photographs on page 2 shows the earth? Talk about the clues which helped you to decide.

2 Make a list of the colours you can see in the picture of the earth on this page. Say what you think each one shows.

▲ *A picture of the earth from space.*

Are all landscapes the same?

The land slopes down from the highest mountains, across hills and valleys, to the sea. The shape of the land is called the landscape.

Landscapes are formed very slowly over millions of years. Mountains are worn away by snow, ice, wind and rain. In other places, the land is rising. Geographers study how these changes happen.

Mountains
Mountains are steep and rugged places. Rocky crags lead to snowy peaks. There is only a little soil to help plants grow. The weather is often bad.

▼ *The Himalayas in Asia.*

mountains

plateau

Using the evidence

1. Which of these landscapes could be used for (a) rock climbing (b) farming?

2. Write down the words from these two pages which describe a landscape.

3. Start a landscape word book. Make a drawing to go with each word in your collection. Keep on adding new words as you find them.

▲ *A plateau in the Andes, South America.*

Plateaus
A plateau is a fairly flat piece of land high up in the mountains. Many plateaus are dry and windy places. Sometimes there are lakes.

▲ Hills and valleys in France.

Hills and valleys
Hills have steep slopes but are not as high as mountains. There is enough soil for grass and trees to grow. Rivers cut into the land making valleys.

▲ A coral island in the Pacific Ocean.

Islands
Islands are areas of dry land which are surrounded by water. They are often found in groups.

hills and valleys
lowland and plain
coast
islands

Lowlands and plains
Lowlands and plains are flat and gentle landscapes. Many people live in lowland areas because they have the best farmland.

▼ Fields in Oxfordshire, southern England.

Coasts
The coast is where the land meets the sea. Some coasts are made up of rocks and cliffs. Other coasts have long sandy beaches, marshes or swamps.

▼ The rocky coast of South Wales.

5

What is the landscape like in the British Isles?

The British Isles are made up of mountains, hills and lowlands. Most of the mountains are in the north and west. There are lowlands in the south and east.

Look at the map carefully. Can you find where you live? Do you live in the mountains, hills or lowlands?

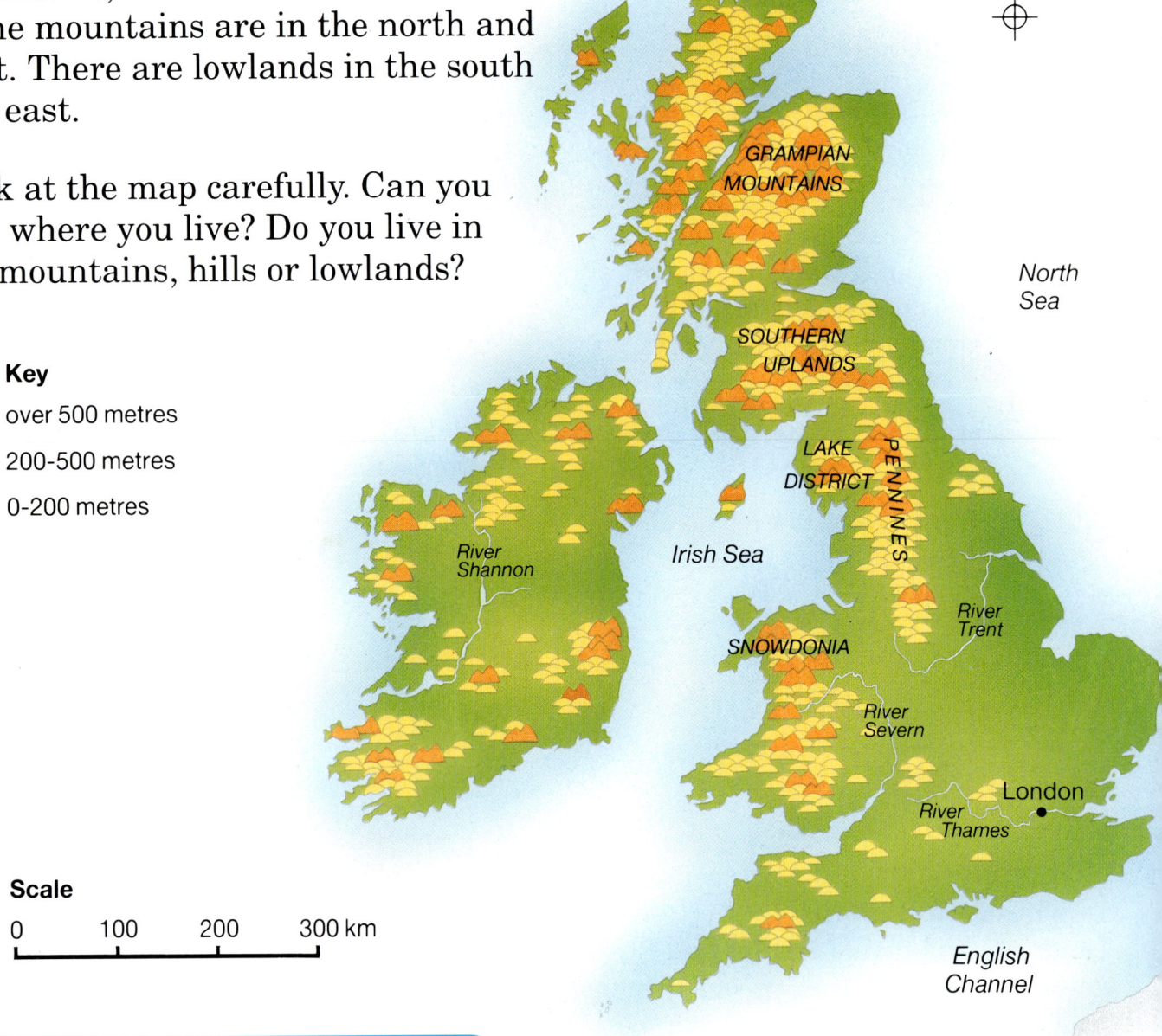

Key
- over 500 metres
- 200-500 metres
- 0-200 metres

Scale
0 100 200 300 km

Mapwork

Use the map to help you answer these questions.
a) What are the names of five mountain ranges?
b) What are the names of four rivers?
c) What other things are shown on the map?

Things to do

Make a scrapbook showing different landscapes in this country. You could use postcards or cut out pictures from magazines. Say which part of the British Isles each one shows and write a sentence about the landscape.

A local enquiry

At St Mary's School the children did a project about their local landscape. First they imagined there were no buildings. Then they made a big plan of the area around their school. Next they added words naming the features that they knew.

Working from their plan, the children wrote down a list of landscape words. Then they drew lines linking these to a list of describing words. Finally they wrote a report about their area. It described what the landscape was like.

> Our school is close to the seashore. Some of the land is wet and marshy. The road out of town goes up a steep hill. Some children live near the downs. As you go inland there are fields and farms. In some places are woods.

You could do a similar project on the place where you live.

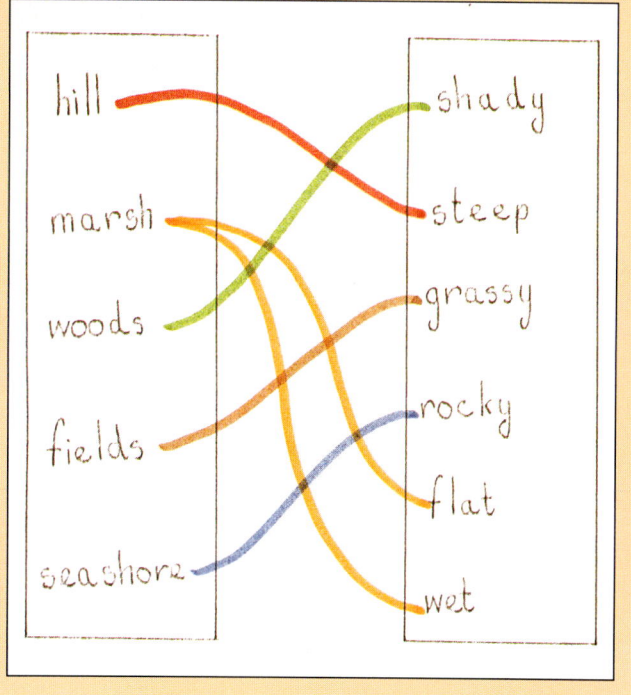

You have learnt

- that the earth is a planet with continents and oceans
- about features of the landscape
- how to study the local landscape.

A Wet Planet

Where do we find water?

Almost three-quarters of the earth's surface is covered by water. Most of it is in the seas and oceans.

There is also a lot of water on the land. There is water in ponds, streams, rivers and lakes.

Wherever you live, water is all around you. It is in the rocks and soil under your feet. Water is also in the air and forms clouds above your head.

Talking and writing

1. Talk about the different places where you can see, hear and feel water.

2. Using the photographs on these two pages, make a collection of all the water words you can think of. Put them into two sets, liquid and solid.

▲ The Victoria Falls are on the River Zambezi in Africa. The falls are nearly 2 kilometres wide and over 100 metres high. The local name 'Mosi-oa-Tunya' means 'The Smoke That Thunders'.

Clouds are made up of millions of tiny water droplets.

Water comes in three forms.

Liquid
The water droplets join together to make rain.

Gas
An invisible gas called water vapour fills the air around you.

Solid
If the air is very cold, the water droplets in clouds turn into snow or ice.

Rain fills the dips and hollows in the land to make lakes.

Snow can turn into rivers of ice called glaciers.

Rivers run down slopes to the sea.

Icebergs are huge blocks of ice floating in the sea.

All the water ends up in the sea.

Why is water important?

Without water everything would die. Trees and plants need water from the soil. People and animals use water for drinking and keeping themselves clean. Fish and many other animals need to live in water.

Apples and other fruit are mostly water.

Birds visit ponds to find water to drink. They also use water to clean their feathers.

Most plants need lots of water to grow well.

Fish live in water. If ponds dry out they die.

Tree roots take water from deep down in the soil.

Ants can live longer without water than any other animal.

Worms and insects need water to digest their food.

10

Using water

Drinking and cooking

Washing and cleaning

Watering plants

Travelling

Fact file

- Rain washes salt out of rocks and soil to make sea water salty.
- Each person in this country uses about 150 litres of water a day.
- Water makes up about three-quarters of our body weight.

Using the evidence

1. Look at the picture of the pond on the opposite page. Make a list of plants and animals which (a) use water from under the ground, and (b) use the water in the pond.

2. Look at the photographs. Write down the headings for the four uses of water. Make your own drawings to show how people use water in this country.

How is water shown on maps?

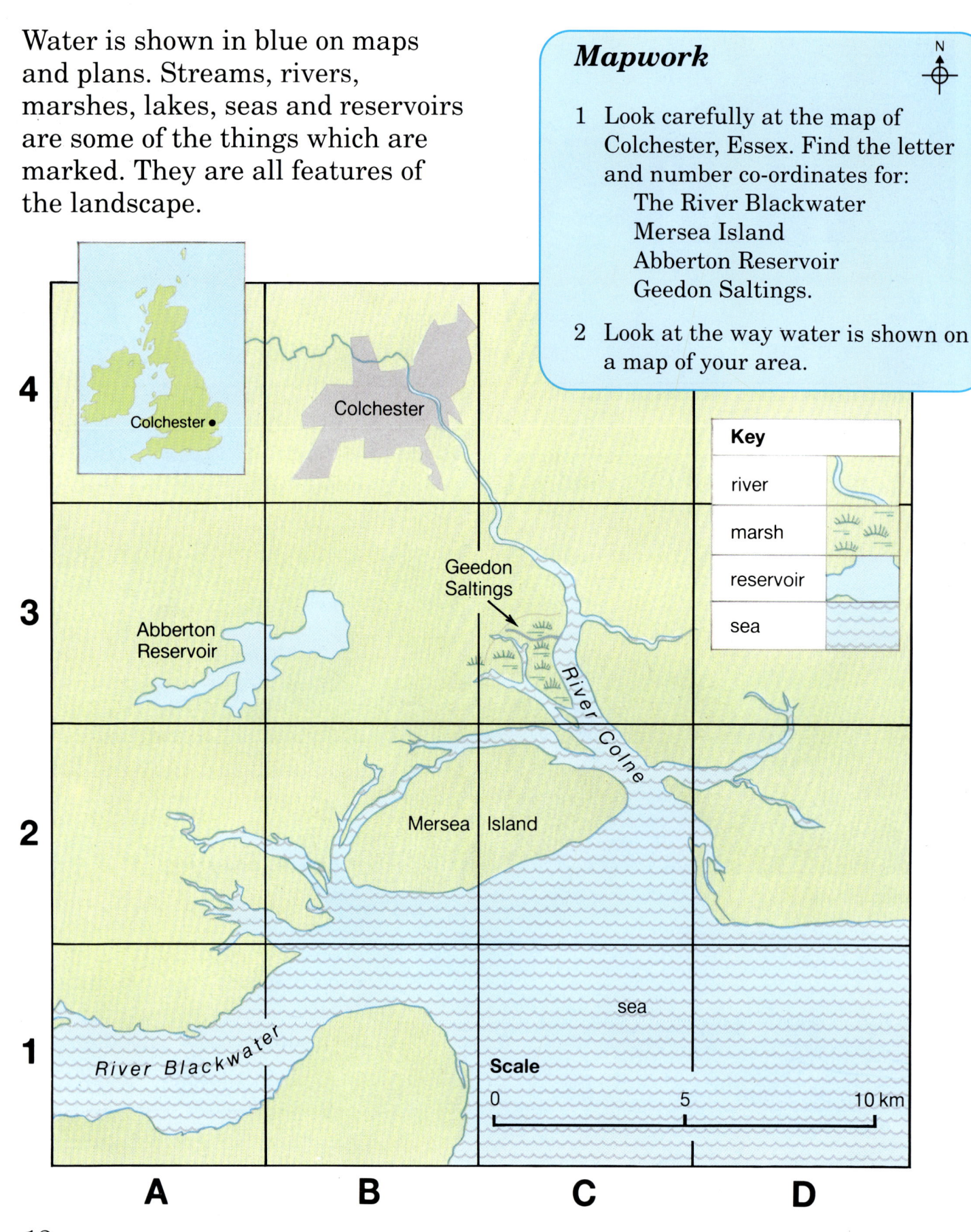

Water is shown in blue on maps and plans. Streams, rivers, marshes, lakes, seas and reservoirs are some of the things which are marked. They are all features of the landscape.

Mapwork

1 Look carefully at the map of Colchester, Essex. Find the letter and number co-ordinates for:
   The River Blackwater
   Mersea Island
   Abberton Reservoir
   Geedon Saltings.

2 Look at the way water is shown on a map of your area.

Closer to home

When rain reaches the ground it flows down hills and slopes. It can:

- run into streams and rivers
- stand in ponds and puddles
- soak into the soil
- go back into the air.

The rain falls from the clouds.

It runs off the roof and into the gutter.

The rain is used by trees and plants.

It flows down the downpipe.

The rain collects in ponds and puddles.

It goes down the drain.

The rain soaks into the ground.

The rain runs into streams.

Things to do

1. Find out what happens to the rain which falls on the roof of your school.
2. When it rains, think about where the water goes. Make drawings of all the different places it goes, in and around your school.

You have learnt

- about the different forms of water, where water is found, and where it goes
- why water is important to animals, plants and people
- how water is shown on maps.

Hot and Cold Places

Is the weather the same all over the world?

There are different types of weather around the world. Some places are very hot. Others are cold. In some places it rains a lot. In others it is very dry.

The pattern of weather over a number of years is called the climate. The photographs on these two pages were taken in a rainforest, a desert and in polar lands. Each place has its own climate.

Fact file

- Even in one square kilometre of rainforest there are 40,000 types of insect.

- The Sahara desert is the world's largest desert. It is over 5,000 kilometres across.

- The north pole and Antarctica are covered by vast sheets of ice.

Rainforest
In the rainforest the weather is always hot and wet. Huge numbers of plants and animals live in the trees. Wide rivers flow through the forest.

Talking and writing

1. Look carefully at the photographs. If you were lost in each place what would you need to survive? Discuss the problems and say what you would put in your survival kit.

2. Talk about the animals which can live in the rainforest, desert and polar lands. Make a list for each place.

Desert
In the desert the weather is very dry. Plants and animals have to live on very little water. Some deserts are very hot.

Polar lands
Polar lands have the coldest weather on earth. In some places snow and ice last all year. Only a few plants and animals can live there.

How do people live in hot and cold places?

In the past, people found it hard to survive. They had to grow all their food, make their clothes and keep their own animals. They used whatever materials they could find to build their homes. If the weather was too hot or too cold their crops or animals could die.

Today, people can live almost anywhere in the world. Electricity, machines and modern houses help us to cope with difficult weather. Food can be delivered by lorry or by plane.

However the weather can still affect the way people live, especially in very cold or very hot places.

Using the evidence

1. Look at the pictures of the desert. Make a drawing of (a) a building, (b) a plant or animal, (c) something people do.

2. Now look at the pictures of the polar lands. Make some more drawings.

Living in polar lands
In Greenland most people earn a living from fishing. What do you think is happening in these two photographs?

Living in the desert
There are a few places in the desert where people can find water. These places are called oases. Some oases are small villages. Other oases are towns and have important markets.

▼ *An oasis in the Sahara desert.*

Many desert houses are built from local materials such as mud and straw. They have flat roofs because there is very little rain.

In the past, camels were often used to carry heavy loads. Today trucks and cars are more common.

Food crops, like wheat, grow well in the desert when they have enough water.

All life depends on water in the desert.

Date palms grow in the heat of the hot desert sun.

Why are some places hot and other places cold?

At the equator the sun rises high in the sky. The sun's rays are very strong. They fall straight on to the earth and heat it up.

Near the north and south poles the sun is always low in the sky. The sun's rays are weak, shadows are long and the air never gets warm.

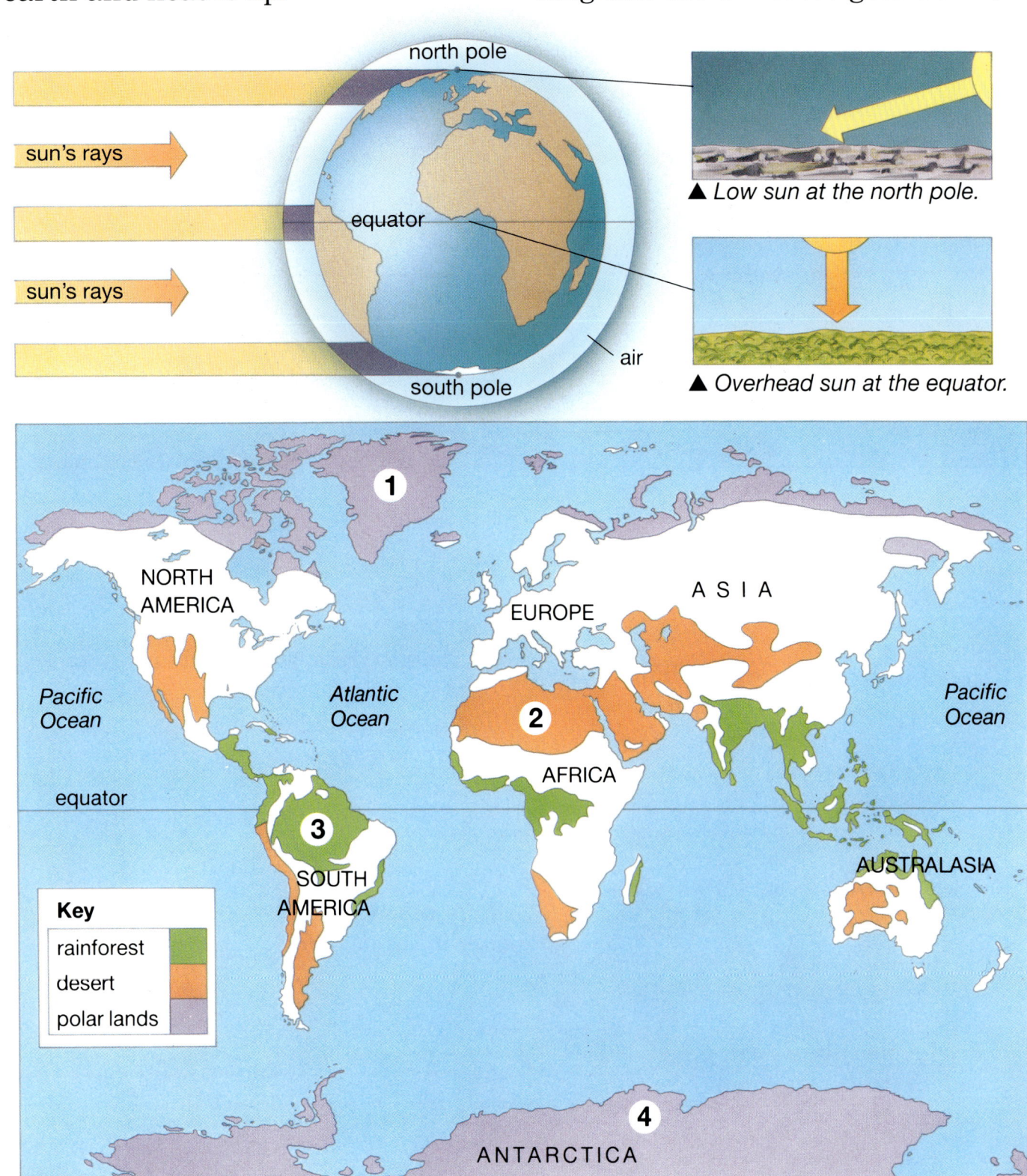

▲ Low sun at the north pole.

▲ Overhead sun at the equator.

Key
- rainforest
- desert
- polar lands

18

Closer to home

In this country we sometimes get hot, dry weather in the summer. The ground dries out and cracks appear. Rivers start to dry up. In the desert the weather is hot and dry nearly all the time.

In winter we sometimes get very cold weather. Ponds and lakes freeze over. Snow covers the land. Plants stop growing and animals hibernate. We have to wear warm clothes. In polar lands the weather is like this even in summer.

▲ *A dried up village pond in July.*

▲ *Snowy gardens in London.*

Mapwork

Look at the numbers on the map opposite, then decide which numbers match the places in this list:

Sahara desert   Antarctica
Amazon rainforest   Greenland

Things to do

1. Decide if these words describe hot weather or cold weather.

   boiling   cool   hot   snow
   burning   chilly   icicle   sticky
   freezing   frosty   mild   sunny
   cold   heat   shiver   warm

   Write them out in two columns.

2. Which places in your school are cold and icy in winter? Which places are hot and sunny in summer?

You have learnt

- that some parts of the world are always hot and other parts are always cold
- why the weather affects the way people live and the plants which can grow
- how to use words to describe the weather.

19

A Place to Live

What is a settlement?

A settlement is a place where a group of people have made their homes close together.

When people start living on other planets they will have to build settlements where they can live safely. They will need to grow food and to make homes where they can live. In the past, villages were built here on earth for the same reasons.

▼ A settlement on the planet Mars might look like this.

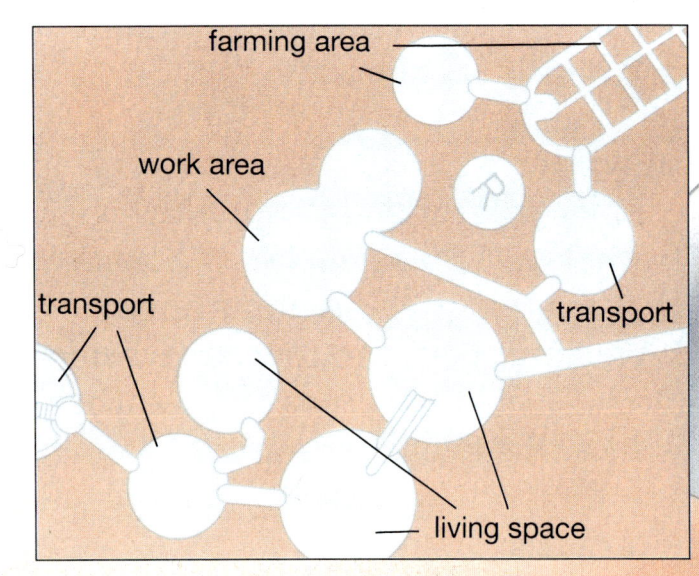

▲ Land use map for a settlement on Mars.

Talking and writing

1. Talk about each of the things shown in the picture. Why are they needed?
2. Which three things do you think are most important for a settlement? What could people manage without?

farming area

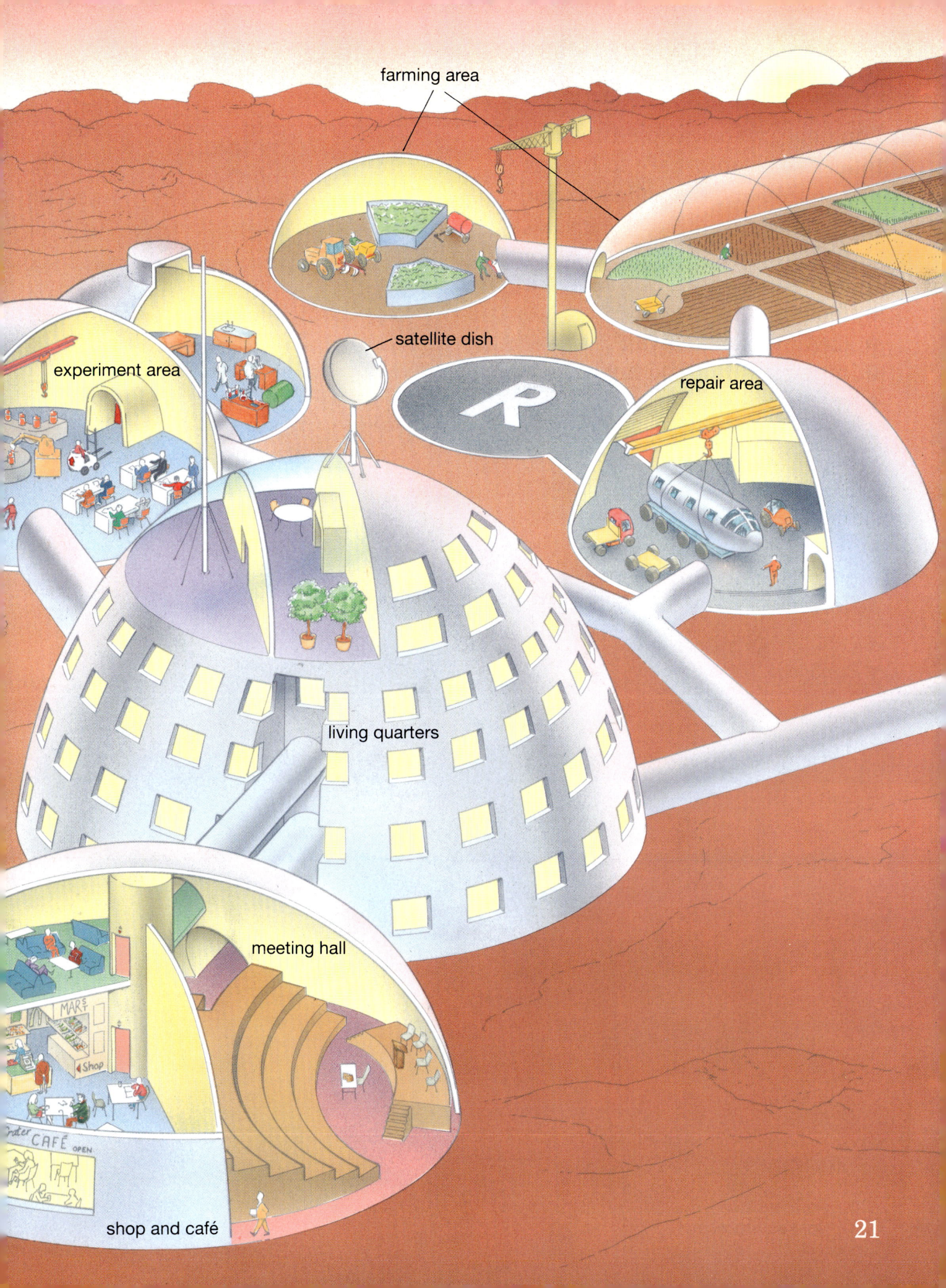

satellite dish

experiment area

repair area

living quarters

meeting hall

shop and café

21

What is a village?

Long ago, when people first began to look for somewhere to live, they had to find the best place to build their homes.

In order to survive people need:
- food to eat
- clean water to drink
- materials to build houses
- a way of keeping warm
- somewhere which is safe.

All over the world people have the same needs. The villages they make look different because the landscape and climate are different.

▼ *Bainbridge, North Yorkshire.*

Using the evidence

1. Write a few sentences saying how people in Bainbridge have used their surroundings.

2. Look at the photographs of villages in other parts of the world. How do the people get food and water? How do they keep safe? Draw a picture of one of the villages and write your answers in labels around the edge.

Labels on illustration:
- stone from the quarry
- village in a sheltered valley
- drinking water from a spring
- hills for grazing sheep
- meadows for hay
- trees provide fuel for keeping warm
- fish from the river
- fields for crops

A desert village
Burkina Faso, West Africa
This village is on the edge of the Sahara desert. The houses give shade and shelter from the sun. They have been grouped together for safety. The walls are made from baked earth and the roofs are made from dried grass. The people keep goats and cattle.

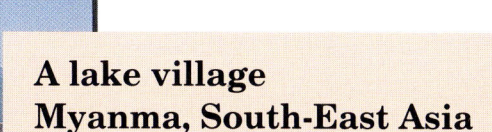

A lake village
Myanma, South-East Asia
The people in this village make their living by fishing. They eat some of the fish and sell the rest in the market. The wood for their houses comes from the forest nearby. The houses are built on stilts to keep the village safe from floods.

A mountain village
Austria, Central Europe
This village is high in the Alps. The winters are cold and it often snows. The houses are made from stone and wood. Their roofs hang down over the walls so the snow can slide down to the ground without blocking doors and windows. Some people in the village keep cows. The cows feed in the high meadows above the village in summer.

How are villages in the United Kingdom changing?

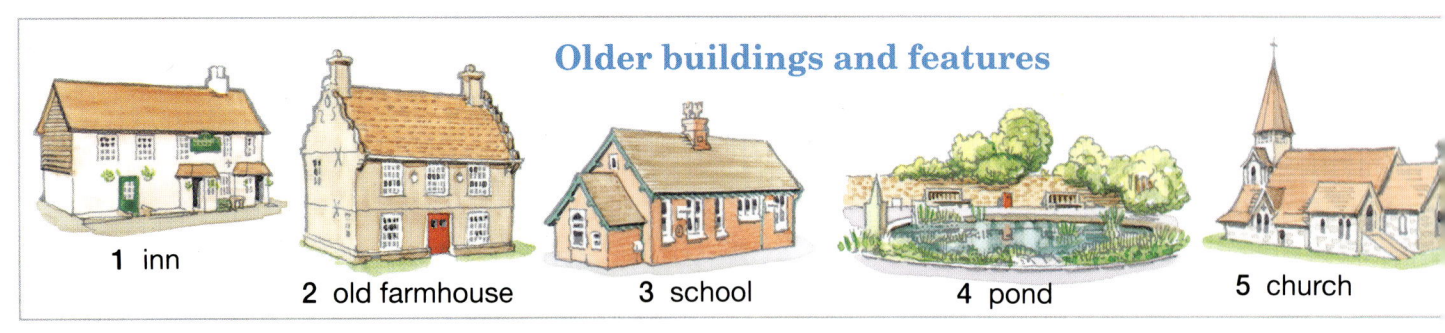

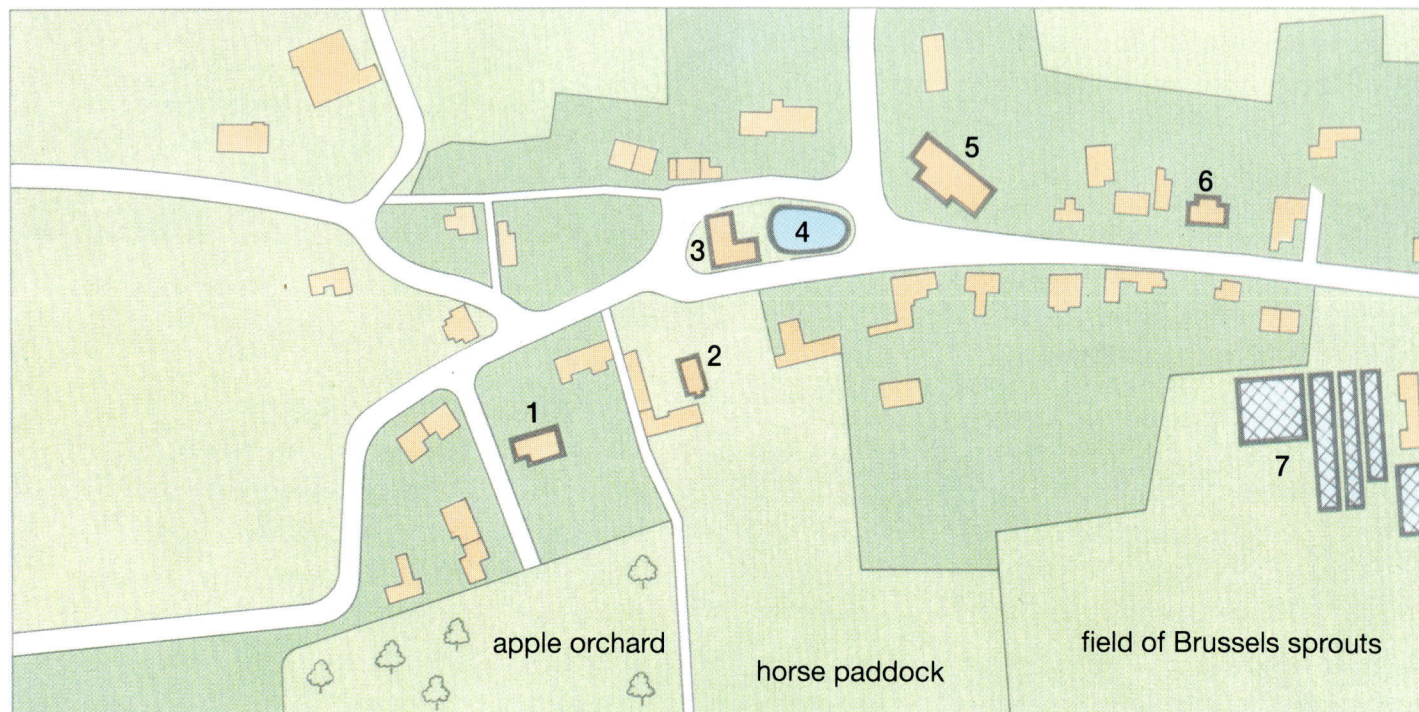

Older buildings and features

1 inn
2 old farmhouse
3 school
4 pond
5 church

Worth is a village in Kent. Two hundred years ago it was a little group of farms and houses around a church and a pond. In Victorian times, houses were added and a school was built.

Worth now has a small shop, a playing field and many more houses. A farmer has built some large greenhouses for tomatoes. The village is much bigger than it used to be, but it still has farmland all around it.

Many villages in the United Kingdom are like Worth. They have grown larger as people who work in the towns have come to live in the country. New houses and roads have been built.

You can explore villages for yourself. If you look hard you can find clues that tell you which buildings are old and which ones are new.

Newer buildings and features

6 shop   **7** greenhouses   **8** bus stop   **9** new house   **10** new bungalow

main road

playing field

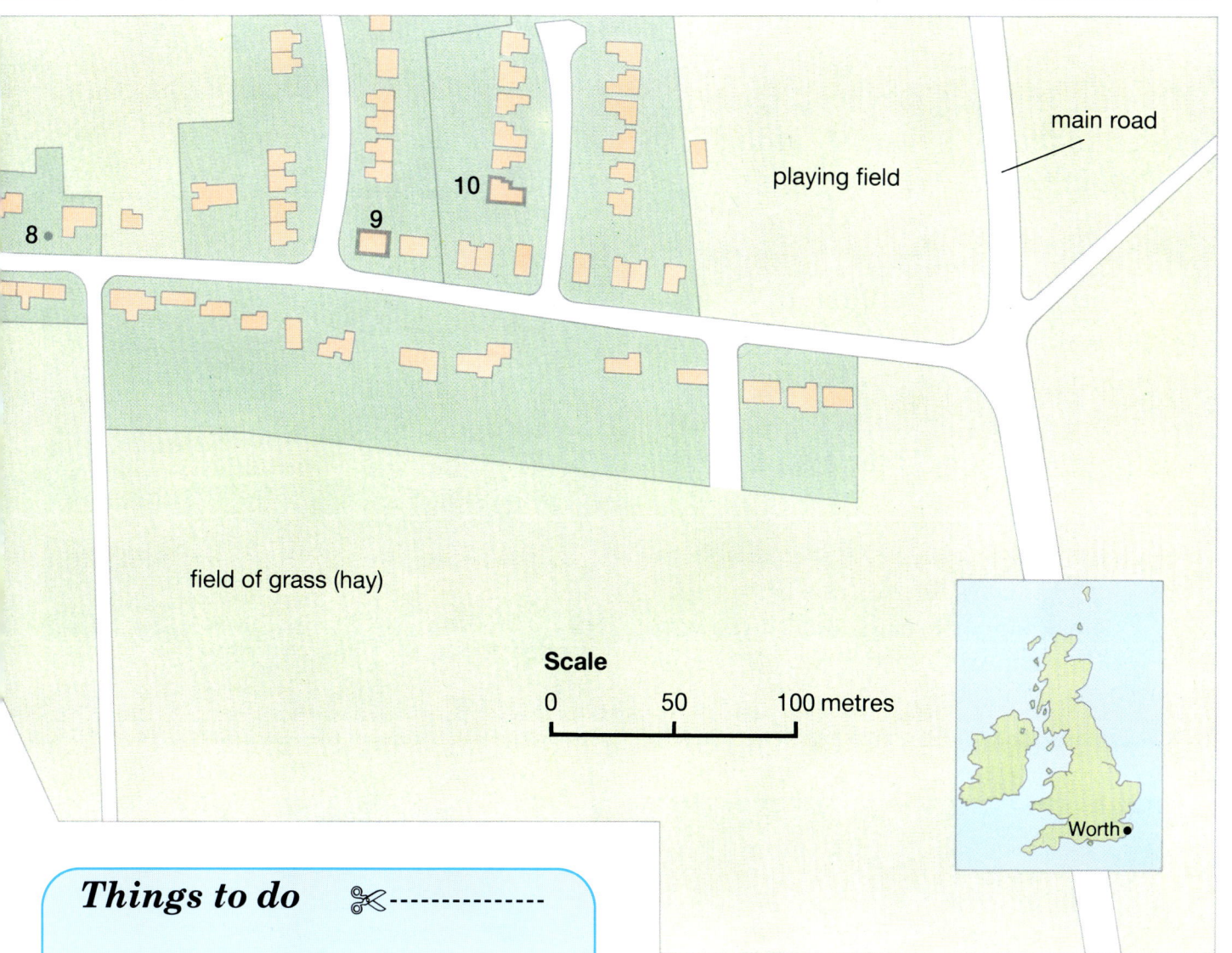

field of grass (hay)

Scale
0   50   100 metres

Worth

Things to do

1. Make a list of the different buildings, features, and crops shown on the plan of Worth.

2. Draw pictures of five buildings in the village. Write under each one the jobs people who live or work in them might do.

You have learnt

- what a settlement is
- about villages around the world
- how to study a village.

Ways of Travelling

What different types of transport are there?

In the past, horses and carts helped people to move from place to place. Sometimes thick forests and high mountains made travel difficult. In many places it was easier to travel by water, along rivers, or across the sea.

In the last hundred years, there have been great changes in transport. People have invented new and better ways of travelling. We can now travel faster and move loads more easily than ever before.

Motor vehicles can move people and goods. Cars, lorries and buses need good, smooth roads and places where they can fill up with petrol.

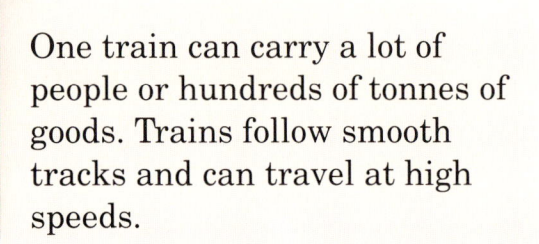

One train can carry a lot of people or hundreds of tonnes of goods. Trains follow smooth tracks and can travel at high speeds.

Ships and boats take people, vehicles and goods across water. All ships need harbours or sheltered places where they can tie up and unload.

Aeroplanes are the newest and fastest way of travelling. They can cross mountains and seas without difficulty. They need airports for taking off and landing.

THE AIR PORT OF LONDON

Talking and writing

Why are different types of transport needed? Which do you think is best?

27

How are people and goods carried from place to place?

More and more people are now travelling by aeroplane for their holidays or work. Aeroplanes are also used to carry goods which have to be delivered quickly.

Airports are big places and need a lot of flat land for the runways. They are usually built on the edge of cities where there is more space.

Lots of people are needed to keep an airport running smoothly. Some people look after the planes. Others help the passengers. People also work in the shops and restaurants.

Control tower
Air traffic controllers help the pilots and give them advice about their routes.

Runway
Planes need long runways for building up speed before take-off and slowing down after they land.

Passenger terminal
The passenger terminal is for:
- checking tickets
- handing in luggage
- changing money
- waiting for take-off
- eating snacks and buying presents.

Tanker
Fuel is pumped from a tanker on to the plane before take-off.

Baggage truck
Luggage is loaded on to the plane from a truck.

Using the evidence

Write down all the different jobs people do at an airport.

Today we need to move lots of heavy goods from place to place. Factories need materials which come from different places around the world. A lot of food that we eat comes from other countries. Lorries, trains and ships are the best way of moving heavy loads.

In Europe and North America lorries carry most of the heavy goods. The goods are packed in containers. There is space for the driver to sleep behind the cab.

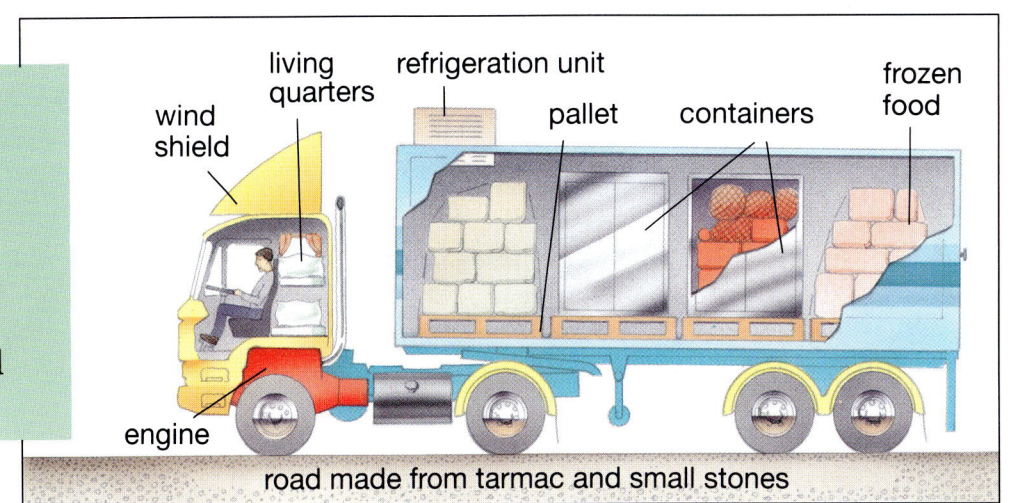

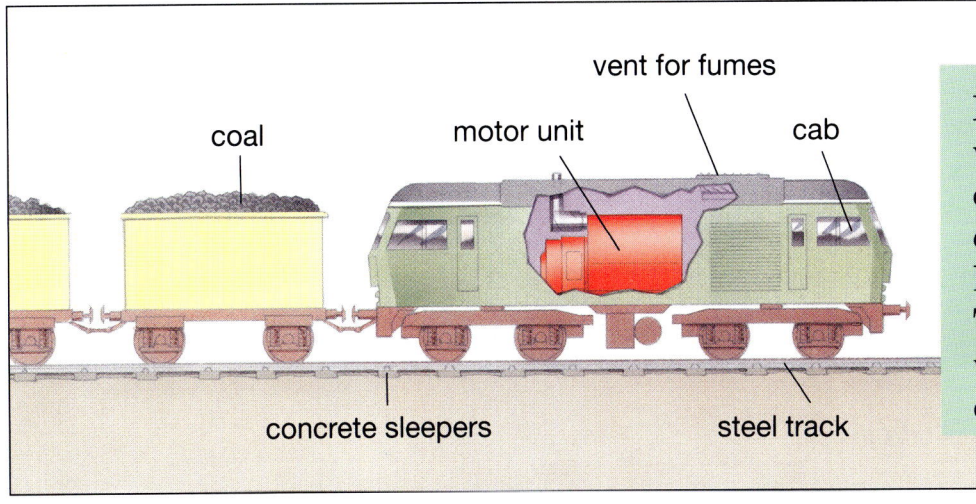

Railways are the best way of carrying goods over long distances especially in countries like China and Russia. The trains are loaded with coal, wood and other heavy loads.

Tankers and cargo ships carry oil, coal, food and other heavy goods. The cargo is stored in the hold. The engine and cabins for the crew are at the back of the ship.

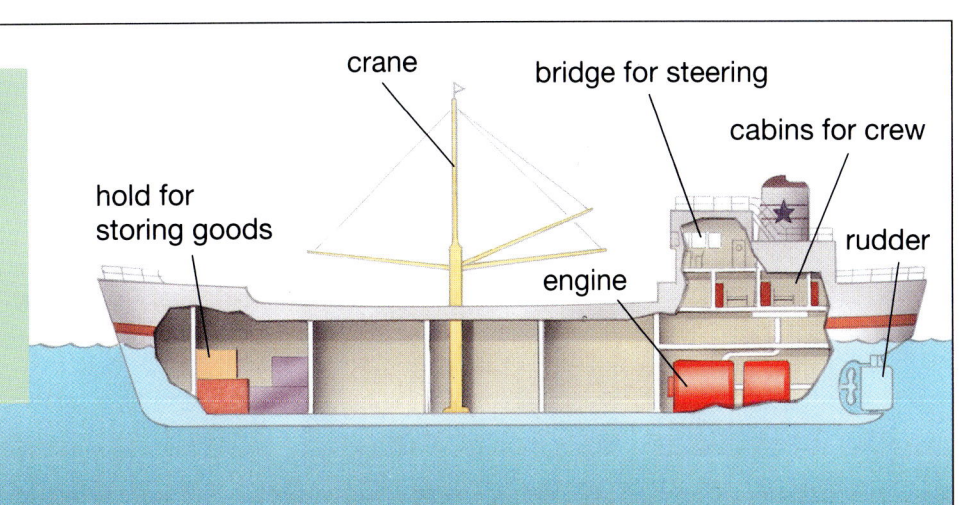

29

A local investigation in the West Midlands

The children of Quarry Bank Primary School decided to find out what types of transport were passing through their area.

They used a map and looked for clues of road, rail, water and air transport. They made notes on the things they found.

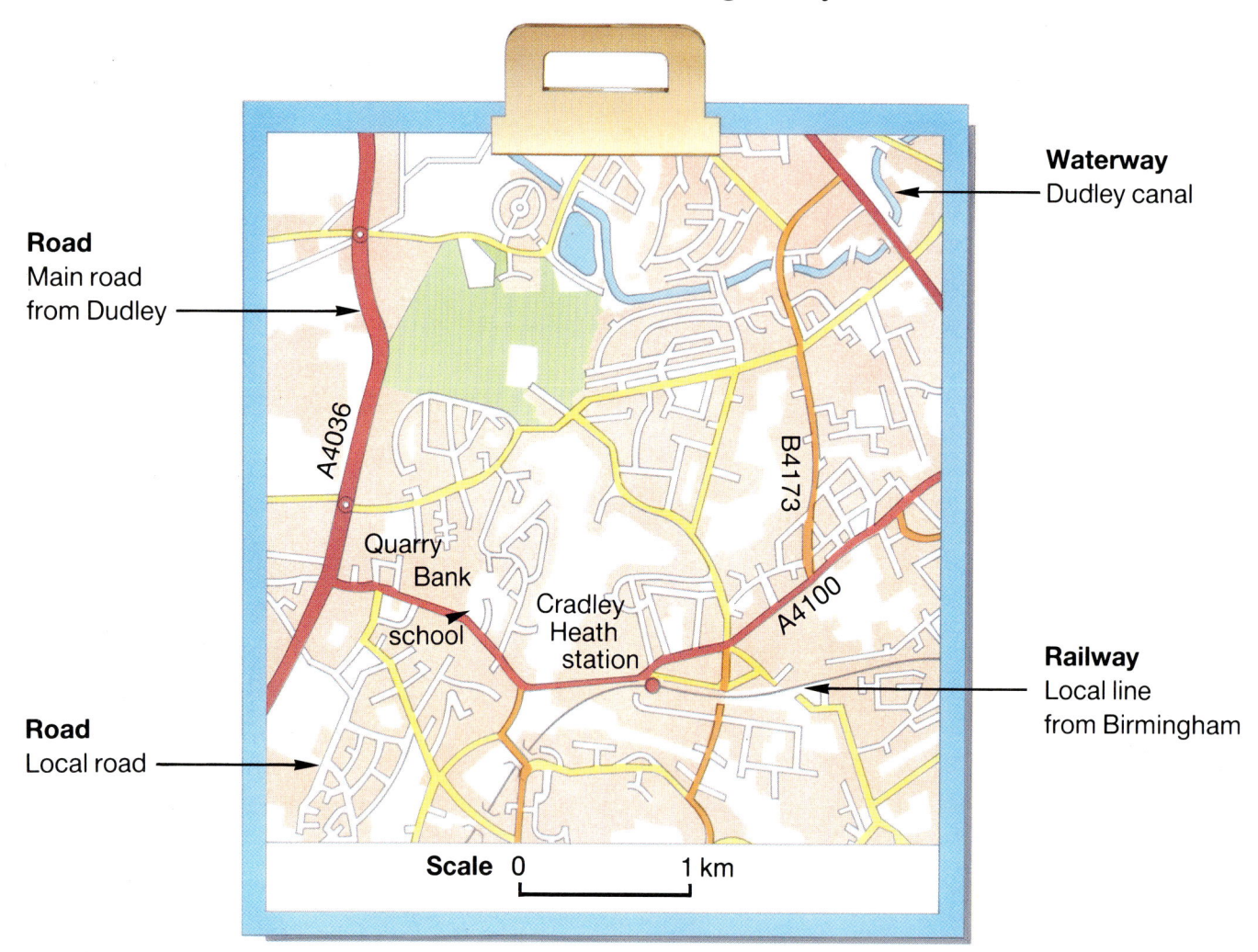

Waterway — Dudley canal

Road Main road from Dudley

Road Local road

Railway Local line from Birmingham

Scale 0 — 1 km

▲ Main roads

▲ Local roads

▲ Railway lines

▲ Canals

The children went on to use the Transport Files (see right). These told them about the traffic which could be in their area.

Finally the children checked if they were right.

◆ They asked the school secretary to telephone the local station to ask about trains on the railway line.
◆ They spoke to a teacher who lived near the canal.
◆ They went out to check the types of vehicle on the main road near their school.

This is the report that they wrote.

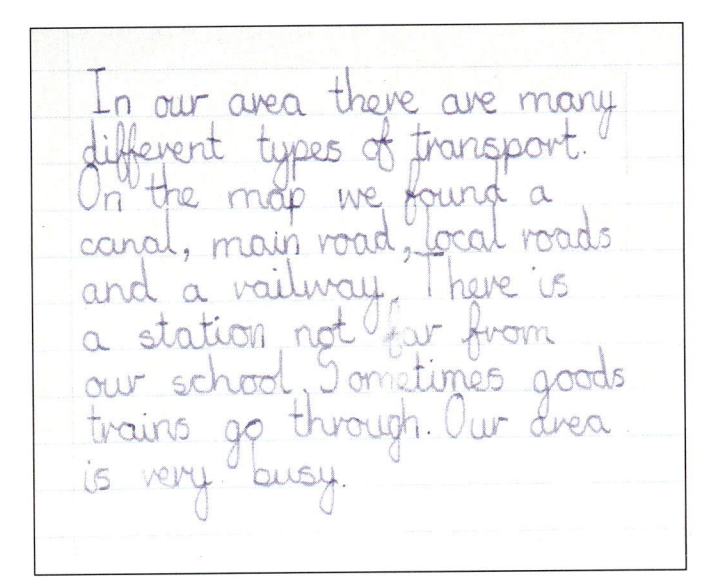

> In our area there are many different types of transport. On the map we found a canal, main road, local roads and a railway. There is a station not far from our school. Sometimes goods trains go through. Our area is very busy.

How to use the Transport Files

1. Find the Transport File you need, eg Waterway.
2. Choose a column, eg Canal. The crosses tell you the vehicles you are most likely to see, eg Barge.
3. Now you can make a list of the traffic you might see in your area.

Waterway

Traffic	Sea	River	Canal
Container ship	X		
Oil tanker	X		
Ferry	X	X	
Fishing boat	X	X	
Barge		X	X
Motor cruiser		X	X

Railway

Traffic	Intercity	Main line	Local line
Intercity 125	X		
Passenger express	X	X	
Local train/sprinter		X	X
Goods train	X	X	X
Metro/underground			X

Road

Traffic	Motorway	Main road	Local road
Lorry	X	X	
Tanker	X	X	
Van	X	X	X
Car	X	X	X
Bike		X	X
Tractor			X
Milk float			X

Air

Traffic	International	National	Local
Jumbo jet	X		
Passenger plane		X	X
Light aircraft		X	X
Helicopter		X	X

Things to do ✂ - - - - - - - - - - -

Look at a map of your own area. Look for roads, railways, canals, rivers and airports. Use the Transport Files to find out what traffic goes through it.

You have learnt

◆ there are different types of transport
◆ why each type of transport is needed
◆ how to study transport in your area.

31

Food and Farming

What is a farm?

Jill and George Wyatt are farmers. They own Brimley Farm in Dorset, in south-west England. George's grandfather bought the farm about 100 years ago.

Half the land on the farm is used to grow grass for cows. Wheat, barley and maize are grown in the other fields. There is also a small orchard and a wood.

There are 100 cows on the farm. They have to be milked twice a day, at 5.30 in the morning and again in the afternoon at 3.30. Every day a tanker calls to take the milk to a creamery. At the creamery the milk is put into bottles and cartons.

There are many jobs to do at Brimley Farm. The grass has to be rolled and fertilized to help it to grow. The crops are harvested in July and August. These are busy months for Jill and George.

▼ *George Wyatt with his dogs.*

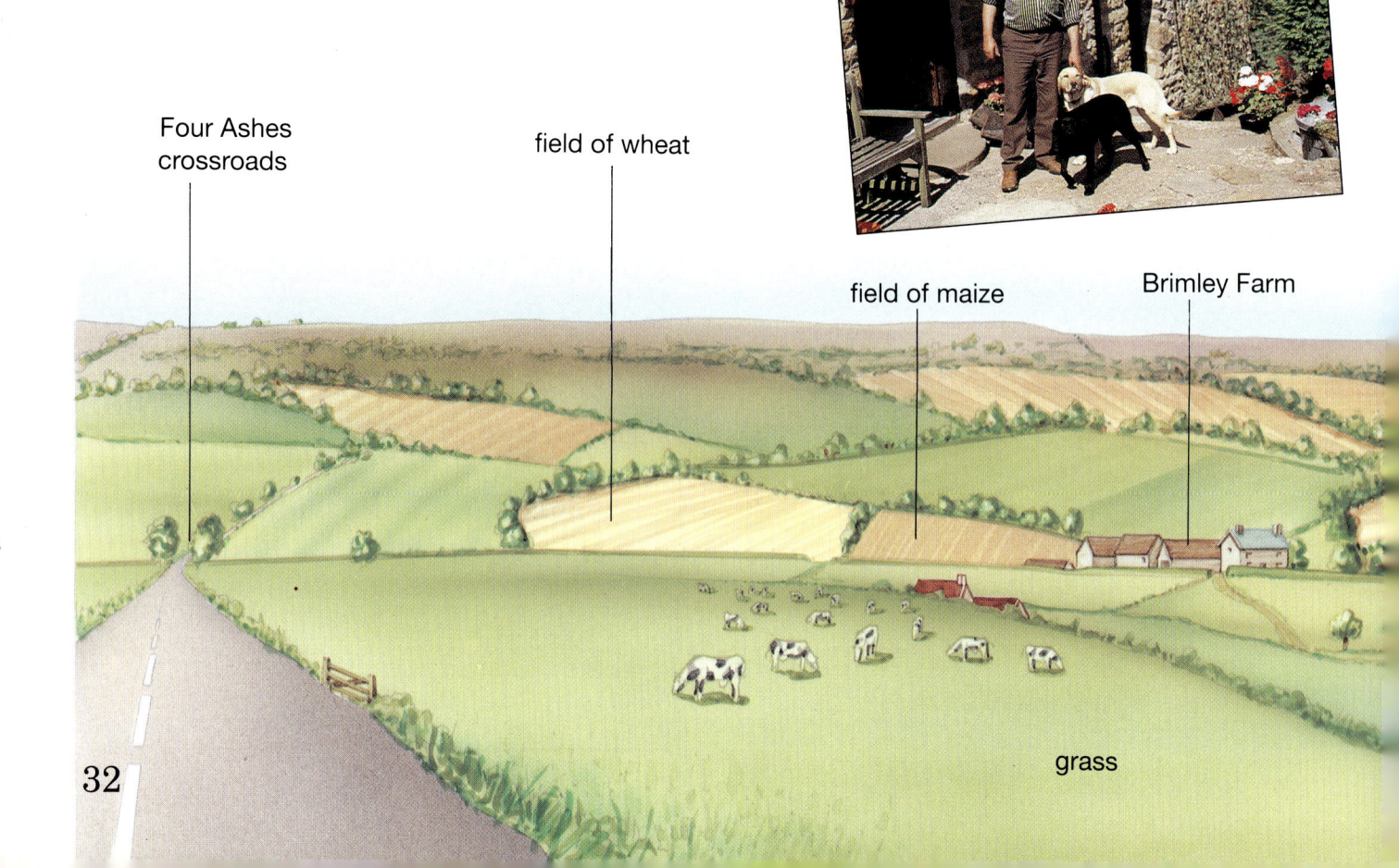

In autumn the fields are ploughed. The farm machines are repaired in the winter, and the hedges cut. There are bills to pay, and records have to be kept on how much milk each cow gives.

Jill and George have two people to help them. One of them drives the tractor. The other person looks after the cows.

Fact file

- Each cow produces about 25 litres of milk a day.

- Wheat is ground into flour for bread and cakes. Barley is used in beer making and for cattle and pig foods. Maize is made into breakfast cereals and cooking oil.

- Foxes, badgers and rooks live in the fields around the farm.

Talking and writing

Why do you think being a farmer is hard work?

DORSET

▼ *Brimley Farm, Dorset.*

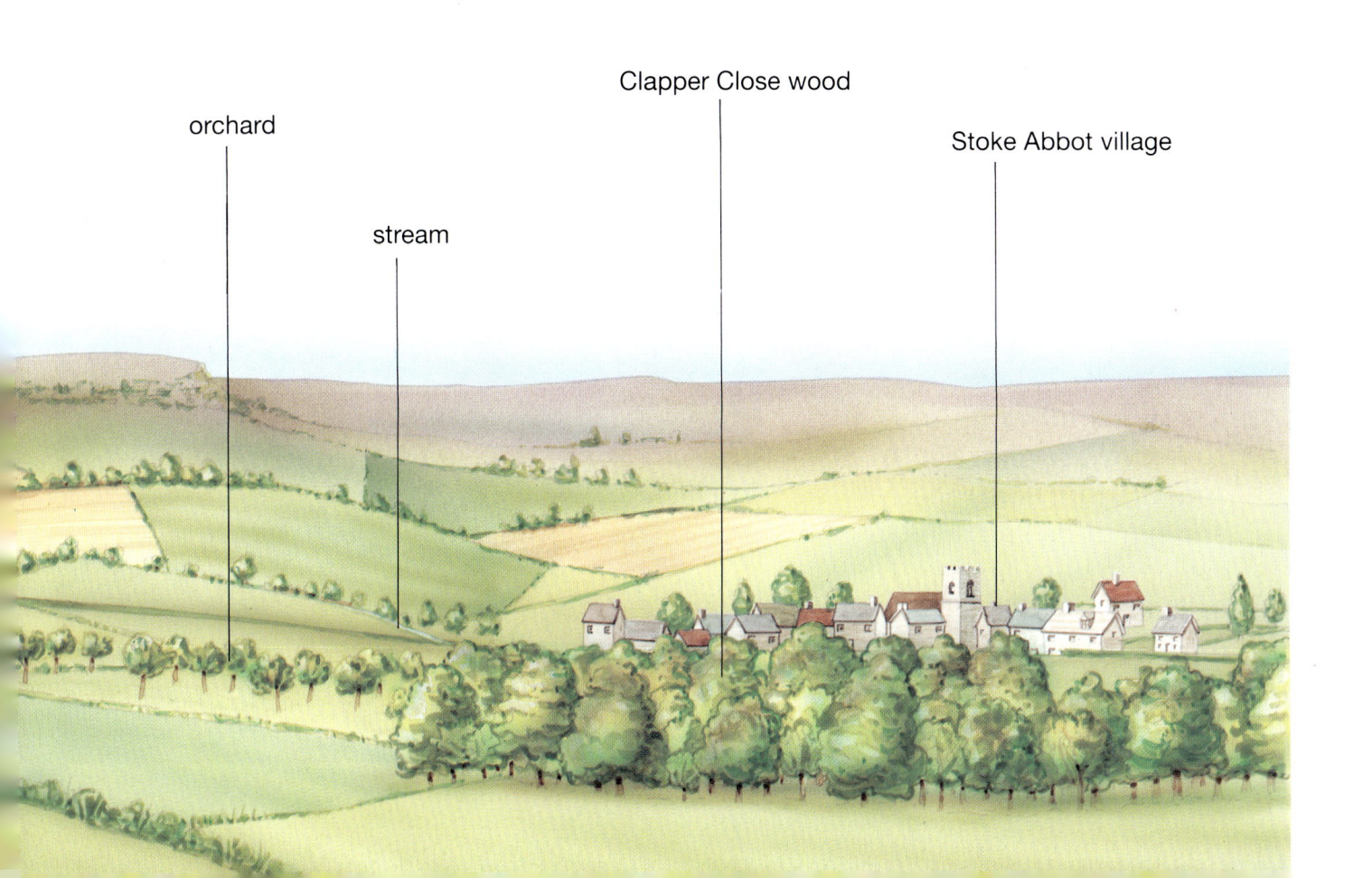

orchard

stream

Clapper Close wood

Stoke Abbot village

Are all farms the same?

Farmers grow crops and keep animals for food. Some farmers just produce what they need for their families and they have nothing to sell. In other places, there are huge farms that sell their products to people in other countries.

Using the evidence

1. How do farmers produce rice, cattle, tea, cacao and apples? Write a sentence about each of the different types of farm.

2. Make up a menu using the food from these farms.

Rice fields

Rice is often grown on family farms in small fields. The young plants have to stand in water while they are growing. Rice is an important food for many people in Asia.

▶ *Planting rice in Bangladesh.*

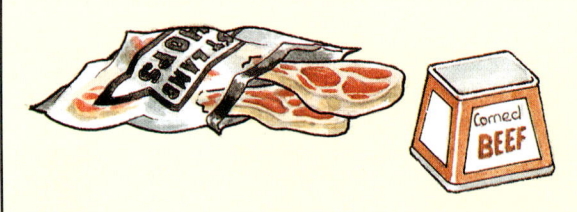

Cattle ranches

In North America, South America and Australia, sheep and cattle are raised on huge farms called ranches.

▶ *A cattle ranch in Australia.*

34

Tea estates

Tea grows on hillsides in India and China where there is plenty of rain and the summers are hot. The tea leaves are picked and then dried.

▶ *Picking tea in India.*

Cacao plantations

Chocolate is made from the beans of the cacao tree. Cacao is grown in West Africa where the climate is hot and wet.

▶ *Harvesting cacao beans in Ghana.*

Apple orchards

Apples are grown in orchards. They need a mixture of sun and rain to grow well. Lots of apples are grown in the United States, New Zealand and France.

▶ *Picking apples in England.*

Why are there different farms in the British Isles?

Some parts of Britain are better for keeping cows or sheep. Other parts are better for growing crops. When farmers decide how to use the land they have to think about four main things.

1 Weather	Is there the right mix of rain and sun?
2 Landscape	Is the land too hilly for growing crops?
3 Soil	Is the soil right for the plants?
4 Market	Will people pay a good price for the produce?

Sheep farms
In the hilly areas of Wales and Scotland many farmers keep sheep.

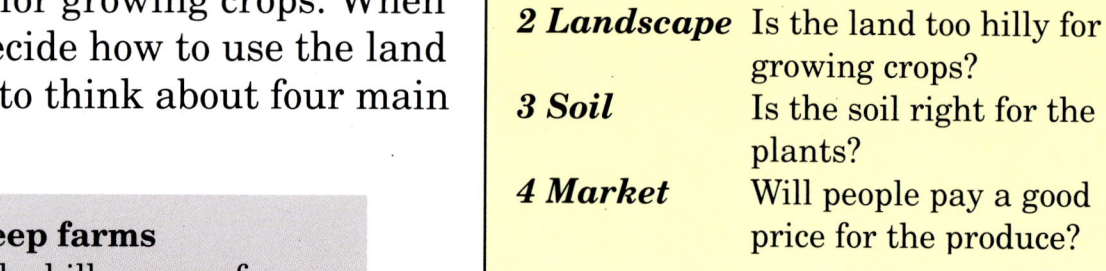

Crop farms
In eastern England the dry, sunny weather is right for growing wheat and other crops.

Dairy farms
In western and central England and Ireland, grass grows well and farmers keep cows.

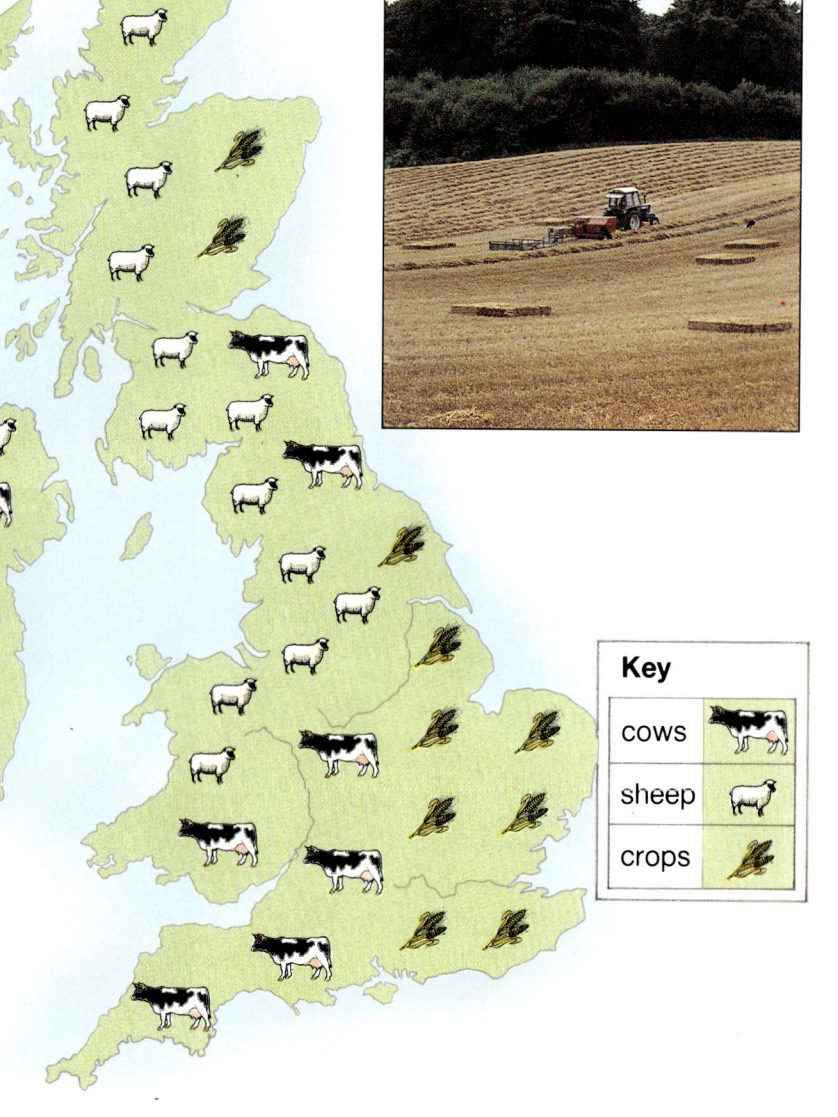

Key
cows
sheep
crops

36

Where does our food come from?

The food in our shops comes from all over the world.

Things to do ✂------------

1. Look at the picture of the shop. Make a list of food which comes from Britain, and food which comes from other countries.

2. Make a display of food and food labels from around the world. Show where each one comes from on a world map.

You have learnt

- that farmers grow crops and keep animals for food
- why there are different types of farm
- that the food we buy comes from all over the world.

37

Environment

Caring for the Countryside

What is a habitat?

The place where plants and animals live is called a habitat. Ponds, woods, hedges, fields, wasteground and old walls all make good habitats. They provide food, water and shelter for the many plants and animals which live there.

Talking and writing

1. Look carefully at the picture and decide where each animal would make its home.

2. Can you think of three animals which would not find the old wall a good habitat?

Looking for a home

butterfly

worm

woodlouse

blackbird

spider

snail

hedgehog

Nettles
Juicy nettle leaves are food for caterpillars and insects.

Old bricks
Old bricks provide shelter for small animals.

38

Branches
Trees have strong branches for nests.

Buddleia
The buddleia (butterfly bush) is very popular with butterflies. They feed on the nectar from the flowers.

Tree trunk
Cracks in the bark make good homes for small animals.

Top of the wall
At the top of the wall there are dry cracks. The bricks can get very hot in the sunshine.

Bottom of the wall
The bottom of the wall is damp and shady.

Earth bank
Some animals live in the soil. Most plants need earth to grow.

Puddle
Puddles provide water for animals to drink.

What are people doing to care for plants and animals?

All over the world people are trying to protect the environment. They want to look after the land and keep the air and sea clean.

In some places, groups of people are working together to stop pollution. New laws also help to protect the environment. However, it costs a lot of money to look after plants and animals and save their habitats.

Colombia
Scientists have special areas where they can study wild plants. If nothing is done to save the plants, they will be lost for ever.

Yellowstone National Park, USA
Some beautiful landscapes have been turned into national parks for people to enjoy.

Antarctica
Antarctica could very easily be spoilt by pollution. All countries have now agreed Antarctica should stay as it is. It is the last wilderness on earth.

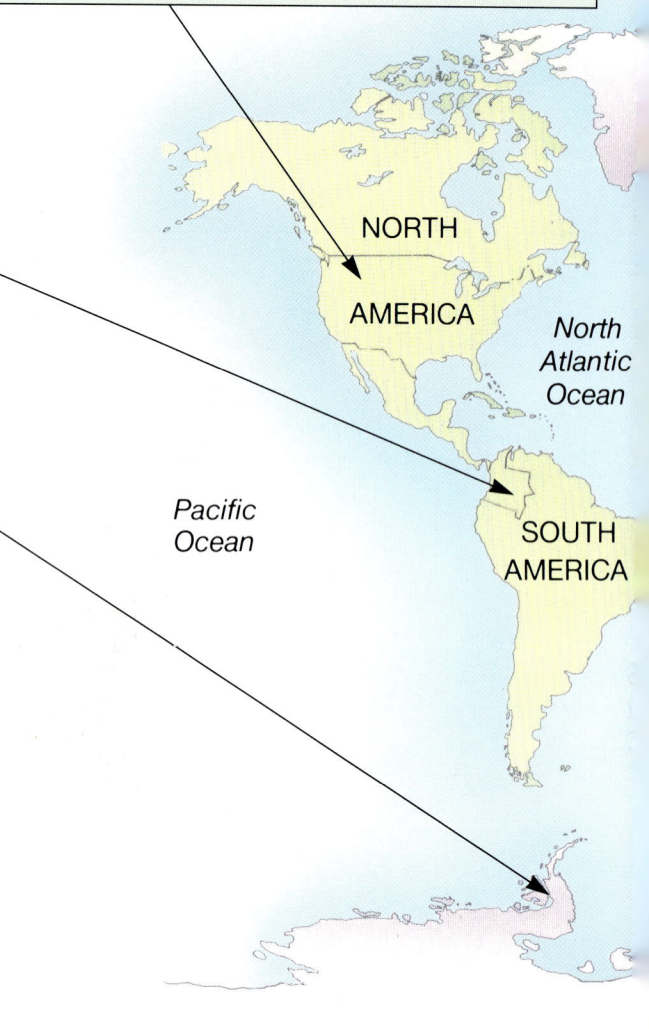

Kenya
Game reserves have been set up for lions, elephants and other animals. In the reserves the animals are protected.

North-West China
Thousands of trees have been planted. The trees stop the desert from spreading over the farmland.

Southern Ocean
People are trying to save whales from being hunted by whalers. If too many whales are killed they will become extinct.

Using the evidence

1. Make a collection of pictures of the plants and animals that are protected by the projects described on these two pages.

2. Design a poster which would make people want to care for the world environment. Give it a slogan.

Nature reserves

In Britain different habitats have been made into nature reserves. This means that all the animals and plants on a reserve are protected.

Michael Walter is the warden of Blean Woods nature reserve. The reserve covers a large wood. Many birds, plants, butterflies and other insects live among the trees.

Michael is always busy working in the reserve. These are some of the jobs that he does every year.

Things to do

Think about each job that Michael Walter does. What would happen if he stopped looking after the reserve?

heath fritillary butterfly

greater spotted woodpecker

Autumn and Winter

Cutting down old trees to make new homes for birds and insects.

Planting new trees.

Planning new work and writing nature trails.

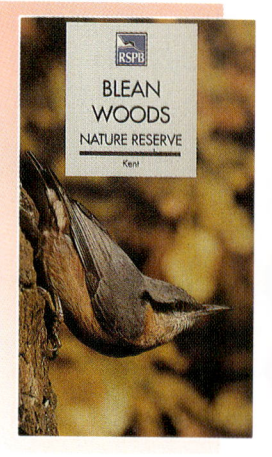

Spring and Summer

Counting the birds and butterflies on the reserve.

Taking visitors on walks.

Clearing spaces for flowers and butterflies.

Blean Woods nature reserve is owned by the Royal Society for the Protection of Birds (RSPB).

Improving the school grounds

At Byron School the children joined a nature club. The club helped them to make their school grounds a better habitat for plants and animals.

▶ *The children designed and made a herb garden.*

▲ *The children put out food to attract birds.*

▲ *The garden is used for school project work.*

Things to do

Look at the photographs. Think of three animals which would like to live in each habitat.

You have learnt

- what makes a habitat
- how people are caring for habitats in Britain and in other parts of the world.

Scotland

What is Scotland like?

Landscape
Many parts of Scotland have high mountains. There are lowlands in the middle of Scotland. The west coast has lots of islands.

Weather
In the Scottish mountains it is often wet and cold. During the winter, snow can cover the ground for many months at a time.

▼ *Autumn in the Scottish mountains.*

Key
- over 500 metres
- 200-500 metres
- 0-200 metres

Scale
0   100 km

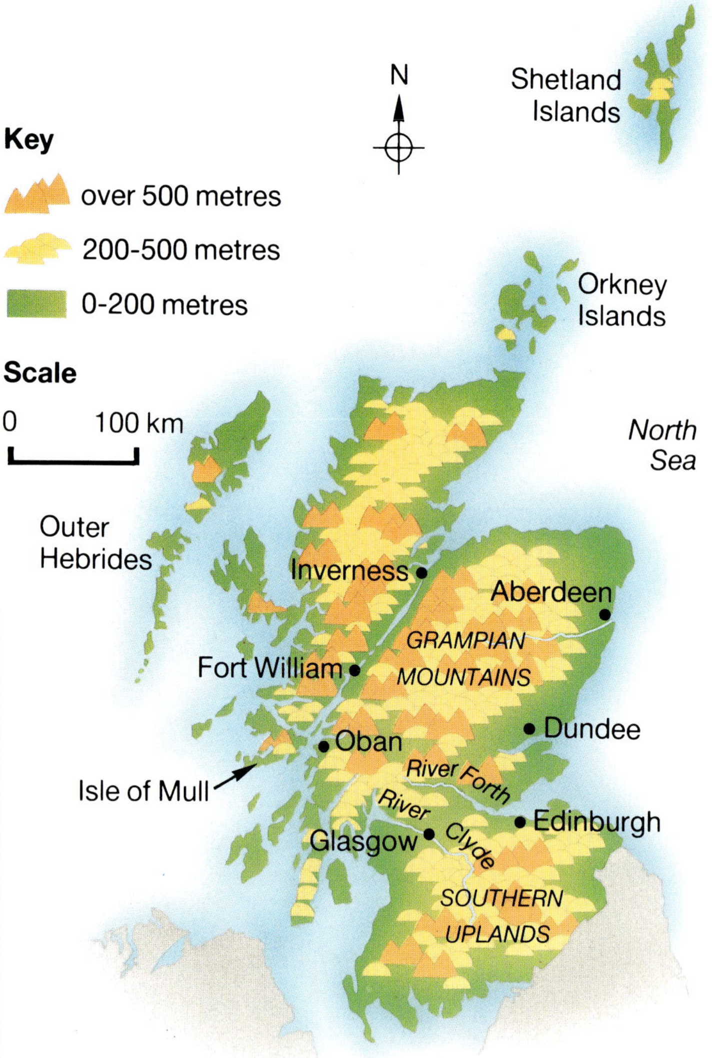

▲ *Scotland is the most northerly part of the United Kingdom.*

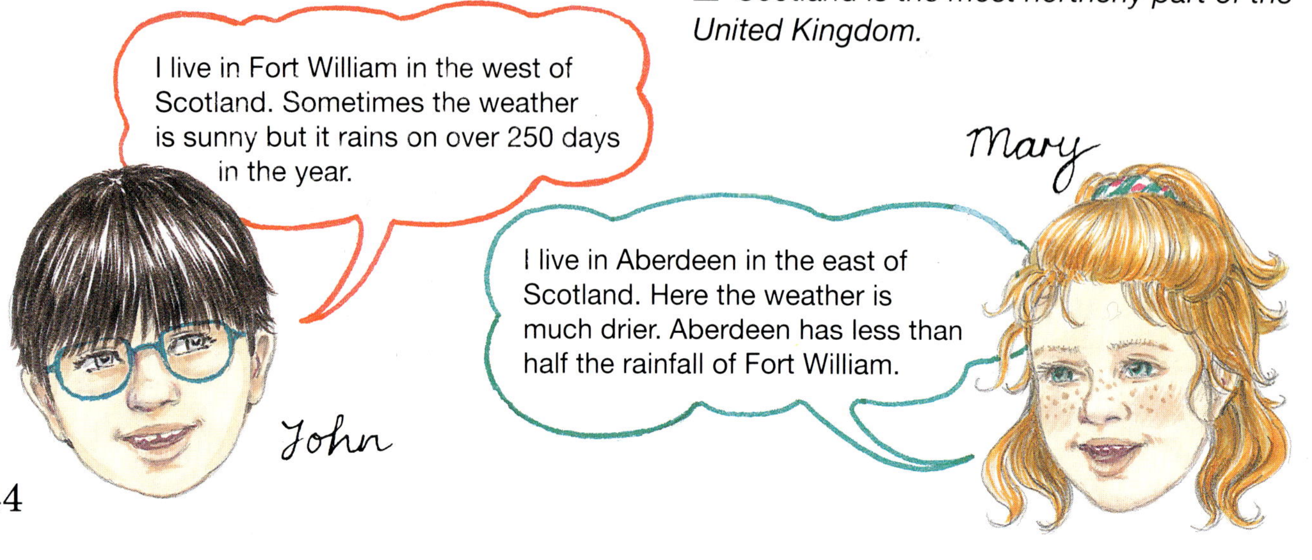

John: I live in Fort William in the west of Scotland. Sometimes the weather is sunny but it rains on over 250 days in the year.

Mary: I live in Aberdeen in the east of Scotland. Here the weather is much drier. Aberdeen has less than half the rainfall of Fort William.

44

Transport

The lowlands and east coast have the main road and rail routes. Ferries deliver food and goods to the islands. There are large airports at Edinburgh, Glasgow and Aberdeen.

Where people live

Most people live in the lowlands of Scotland. Edinburgh and Glasgow are the largest cities. Aberdeen and Dundee are two ports on the east coast. Few people live in the mountains.

▲ An overhead view of Glasgow and the River Clyde.

Talking and writing

Choose ten facts which tell you something about Scotland. Write them on a fact file.

Work

Many people work in electronics, tourism, and the oil industry. In country areas, farming, fishing and forestry are important. Scotland is famous for making tartan cloth and whisky.

▲ There are oil rigs in the North Sea. The oil is pumped up from the rocks under the sea. Then it flows along pipes to the mainland. The people who work on the rig travel to and fro by helicopter.

Fact file

- Two-thirds of the people in Scotland live in the lowlands.
- Ben Nevis (1,343 metres) is the highest mountain in Scotland.
- Oil pollution has damaged some parts of the coast.

Edinburgh - the capital city of Scotland

Edinburgh is a very old city. A castle was built there hundreds of years ago. It stands on a high rocky crag above the city.

Today nearly half a million people live in Edinburgh. They work in the shops, offices and factories.

Edinburgh is a busy place with lots of traffic. People often come a long way to go shopping in the city. Tourists arrive by plane, train and car. They stay in hotels and visit the famous buildings.

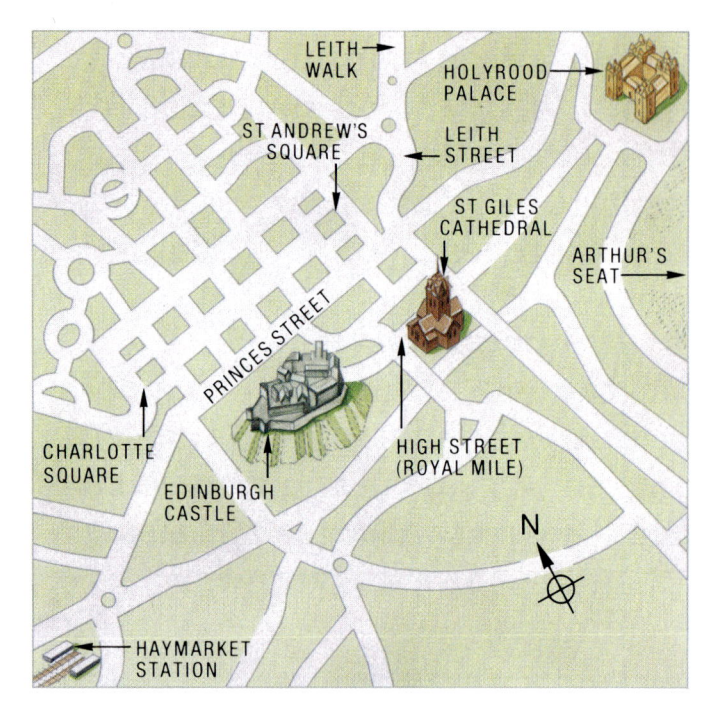

▲ A street map of central Edinburgh.

Things to do

1. How is Edinburgh different from the place where you live? Make a list.

2. Use the street map to follow Isabel's route to work.

3. Make sketches of some of the places you would like to visit in Edinburgh. Give reasons for your choice.

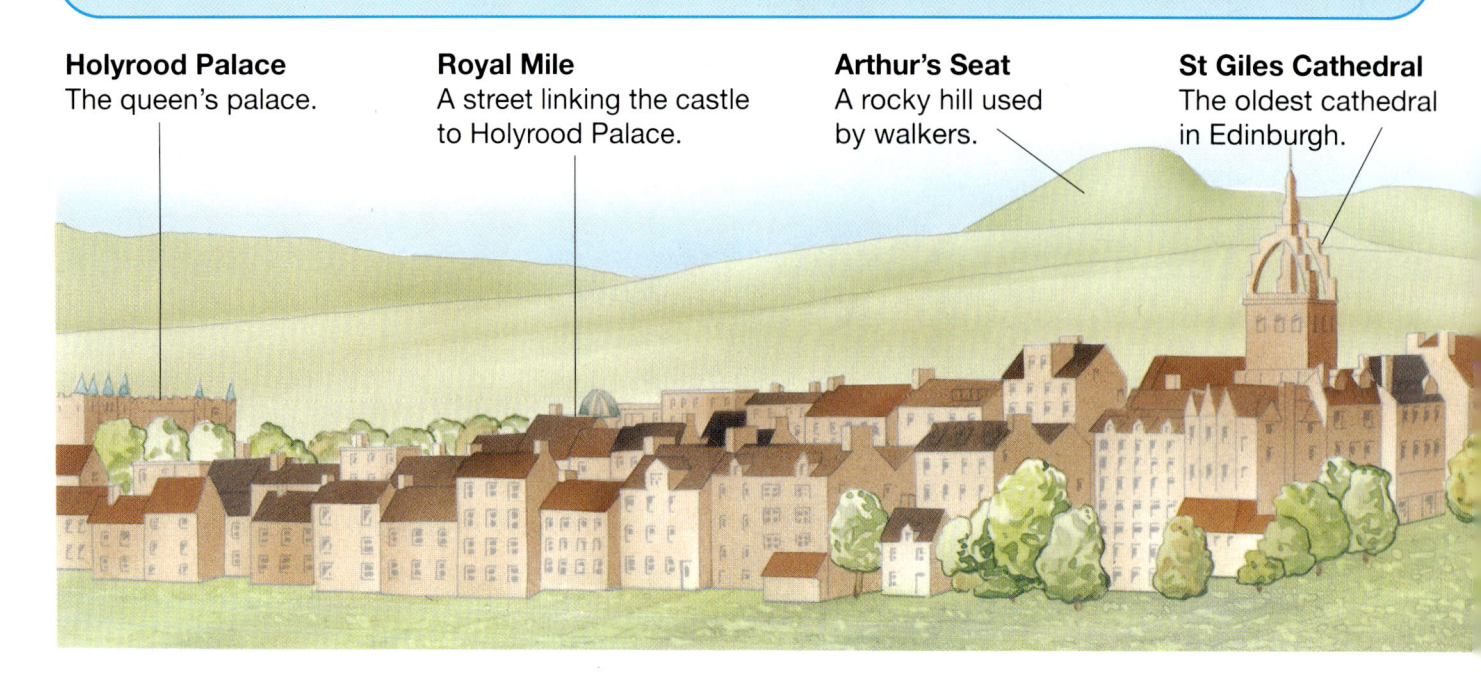

Holyrood Palace
The queen's palace.

Royal Mile
A street linking the castle to Holyrood Palace.

Arthur's Seat
A rocky hill used by walkers.

St Giles Cathedral
The oldest cathedral in Edinburgh.

Going to work

Isabel Andrews is the manager of a bank in Leith. She drives across Edinburgh every day on her way to work.

The first thing Isabel passes is Haymarket station. Next she sees the castle. Isabel drives down Princes Street where there are lots of big shops. Then she follows the signs for Leith. Arthur's Seat, a grassy mountain, is on the right. Finally Isabel arrives at work.

▲ A road and a rail bridge cross the Firth of Forth. The bridges are an important link between Edinburgh and other parts of Scotland.

Edinburgh Castle
The castle used to protect the city from attacks.

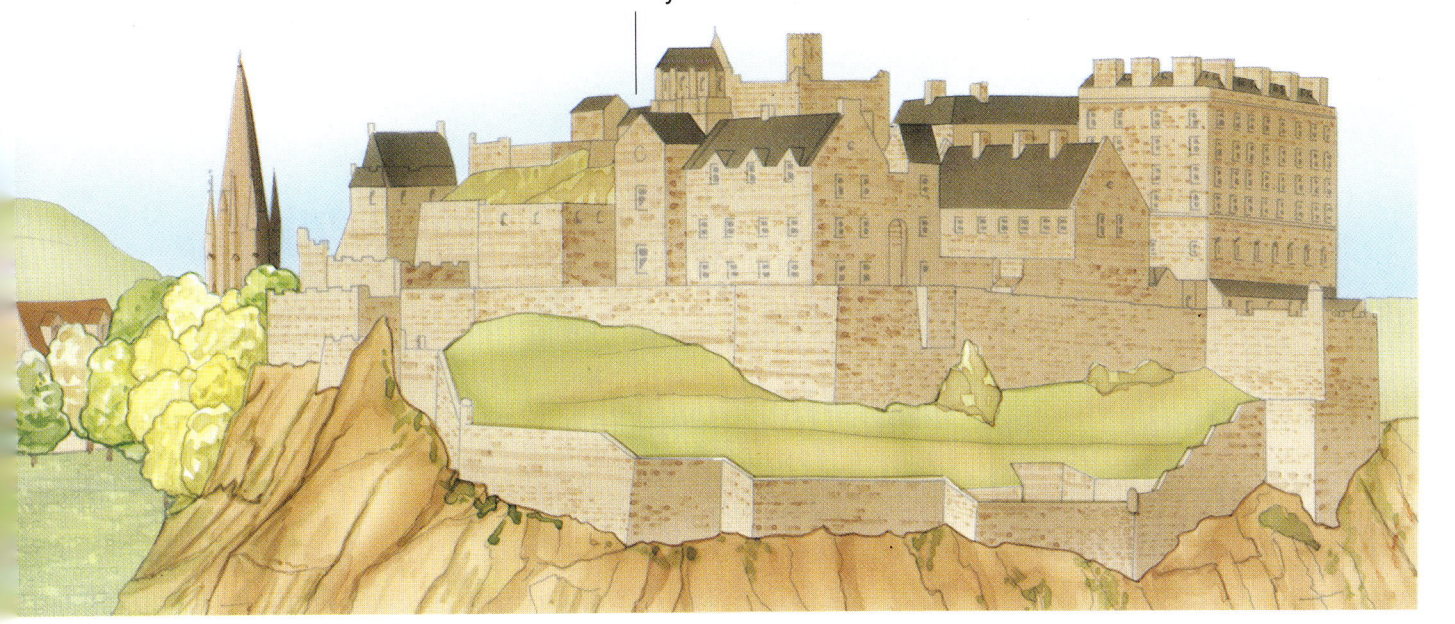

Mull - an island on the west coast of Scotland

Tobermory

Living on Mull

Iain and Morag live on the Isle of Mull. They run a small farm called a croft. A few years ago they moved into a new bungalow. Tourists now come to stay in their old stone farmhouse.

Iain looks after the sheep and cows on the farm. Morag knits beautiful jumpers. She sells them to the tourists who visit the island.

Mull is a very quiet island. There are mountains and moors in the middle and cliffs along the shore.

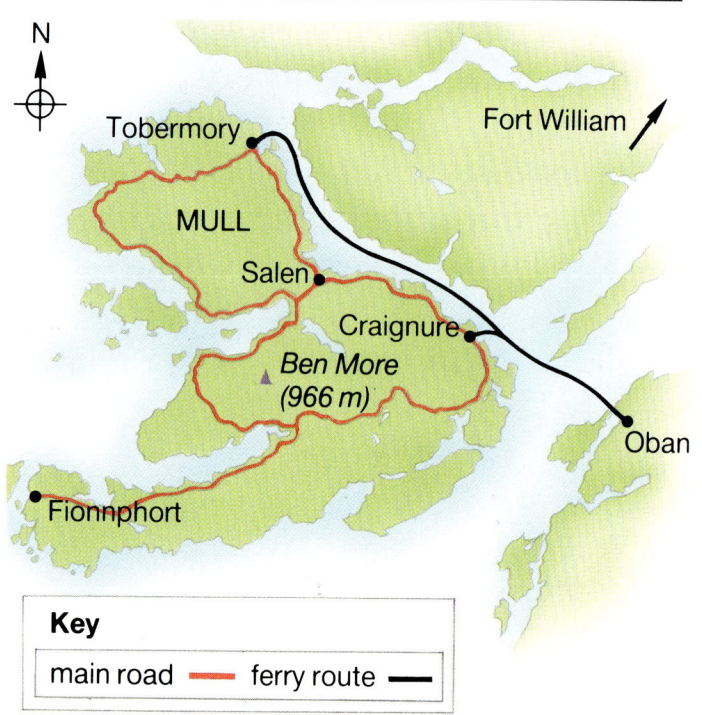

▲ Mull is 48 kilometres from west to east and 42 kilometres from north to south.

▲ Iain and Morag's bungalow.

▲ The old stone farmhouse.

▲ The farm animals.

Visiting Mull

Roy and Christine decided to go to Mull for their holidays. They arrived by ferry from Oban. The ferry was loaded with visitors, food and goods for the local people.

Christine bought a map so they could explore. Roy made sure they had waterproof anoraks in case it rained. They always took a picnic with them as there are very few shops outside Tobermory.

Roy and Christine enjoy bird watching. They carried binoculars with them. The mountains, moors and cliffs are good habitats for plants and animals.

▲ The east coast of Mull.

▲ Here are some of the things Roy and Christine saw on their walks.

Fact file

- About 4,000 people live on the Isle of Mull.
- There are six primary schools and one secondary school on the island.
- Most people live in Tobermory where there are shops and a harbour.
- Over 200 types of bird have been recorded on Mull.

Things to do

1. Draw a postcard showing a scene on the Isle of Mull. On the back write about the things you could do if you were on holiday there.
2. Draw a map of Scotland and label the Isle of Mull.

You have learnt

- about the landscape and weather of Scotland
- where people live
- what people do.

France

What is France like?

France is about twice as large as the United Kingdom. It lies to the south of the United Kingdom across the English Channel.

▲ Skiing in the French Alps in winter.

Landscape
The highest mountains in France are the Alps and Pyrenees. The tops are so cold they are covered in snow and ice all year. The Seine, Loire, Garonne and Rhône are the longest rivers.

Settlement
Large areas of France have only scattered villages and small towns. Paris is the capital city. Other large cities are Lyon, Marseille, Bordeaux, Lille and Strasbourg.

▼ *Nôtre Dame and the River Seine, Paris.*

Weather
The weather in the north and west of France comes from the Atlantic Ocean. The climate is mild and quite wet. In the south the summers are hot and dry. Most of the rain falls in the winter.

Work
France has many industries such as iron and steel, glass and chemicals, cars and aeroplanes, and making clothes. People also work on the land. They produce fine wines, cheese, fruit, meat and vegetables.

▼ *Many kinds of cheese are made in France.*

Transport

▲ *A high-speed train.*

France has one of the most modern transport systems in the world. There are high speed railway lines and motorways.

Talking and writing

If you went on a school visit to France, what could you bring back to make a class display?

The French countryside

Parnac is a village in the Dordogne in the south-west of France. It has a church, old stone buildings and newer houses. The River Lot flows on one side of the village.

Parnac has plenty of sunshine and the soil in the river valley is very good. Many crops are grown in the area.

Grapes are the most important crop. They are made into wine which is sold all over the world.

Some people keep geese and ducks. A type of meat paste, called pâté, is made from them.

The milk from goats is used to make cheese.

Tomatoes, beans and maize are grown for food.

FRANCE
Parnac

There are lots of caves under the ground. Thousands of years ago people used to paint pictures on the walls. Today tourists go to see the famous paintings.

There are many fine old country houses called châteaux in the Dordogne.

The nuts from walnut trees are used in cooking.

Plums, apricots, apples and peaches grow in the orchards.

Things to do

1. Make a list of food that grows in the fields around Parnac.
2. What jobs do people do on the farms around Parnac?

The Renault Clio

Renault is one of the biggest car makers in Europe. It has factories in many parts of France as well as in other countries. One of the factories is in Flins by the River Seine, about 40 kilometres from Paris.

There are lots of towns and villages around the factory. Many of the people who work in the factory live in Mantes-la-Jolie, Les Mureaux and Aubergenville.

▼ The Renault Clio.

▲ Flats at Aubergenville.

▲ The shopping centre, Flins.

▼ The Renault factory, Flins.

54

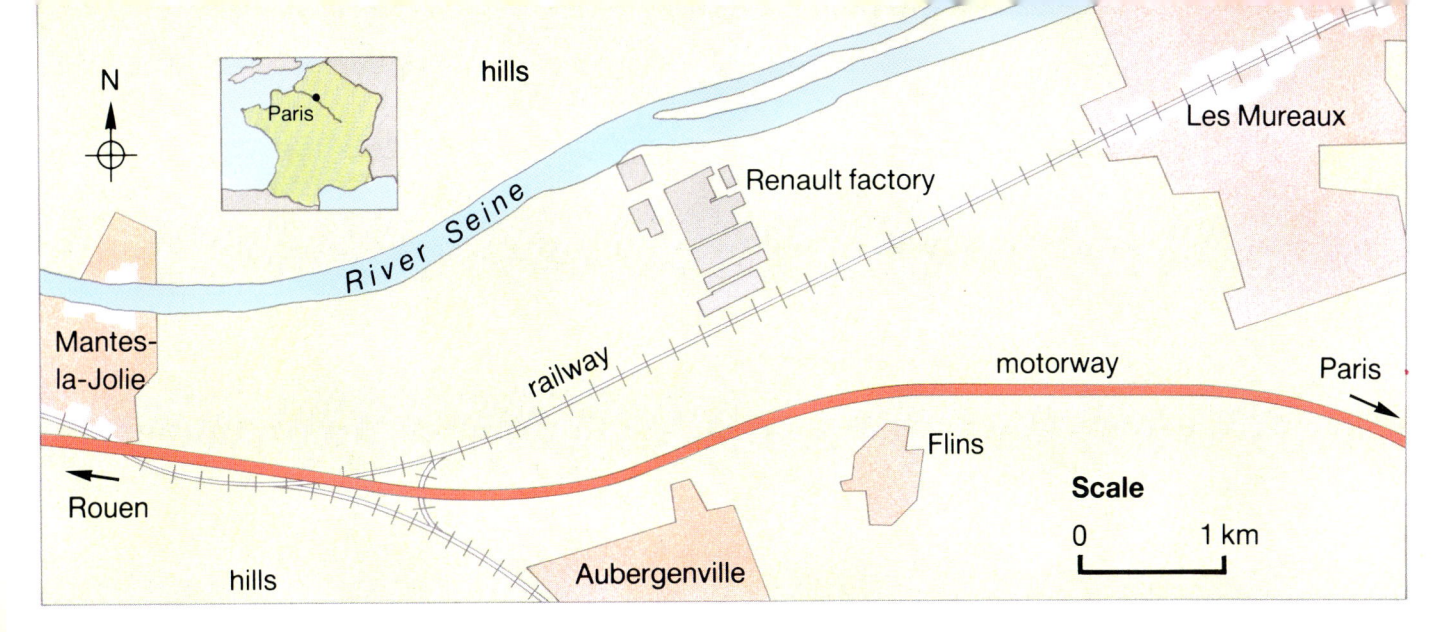

Monsieur Hugo sprays the cars with paint. He travels from Mantes-la-Jolie each day.

Madame Renard lives in Les Mureaux. She checks that the cars are safe.

Monsieur Hassan puts the engines into the cars. He lives in Aubergenville.

Madame Blanc manages the supermarket near the factory. She lives in Flins.

How the money goes round

Monsieur Hugo, Monsieur Hassan and Madame Renard earn their money at the factory.

Madame Blanc has bought a Renault Clio. This helps to make jobs for people at the factory.

They buy their food at Madame Blanc's shop.

Things to do

1. Look at the map on this page. Find out where each person lives.

2. What would happen if people stopped buying the Renault Clio? What would happen to the factory, Monsieur Hugo and his family, and Madame Blanc and her shop?

You have learnt

- about the landscape and weather of France
- where people live
- what people do.

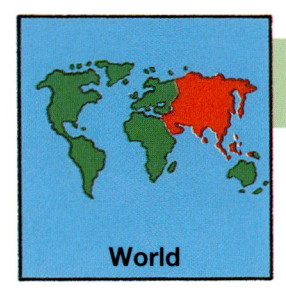

Asia

What is Asia like?

Asia is the largest continent. It is nearly 10,000 kilometres from east to west. In the north the climate is very cold. The south is hot with deserts and rainforests.

More than half the people in the world live in Asia. The largest countries are Russia, China and India.

▲ The Himalayas are the highest mountains in the world.

▲ Shanghai is the largest city in China.

▲ The Gobi Desert is very dry and rocky.

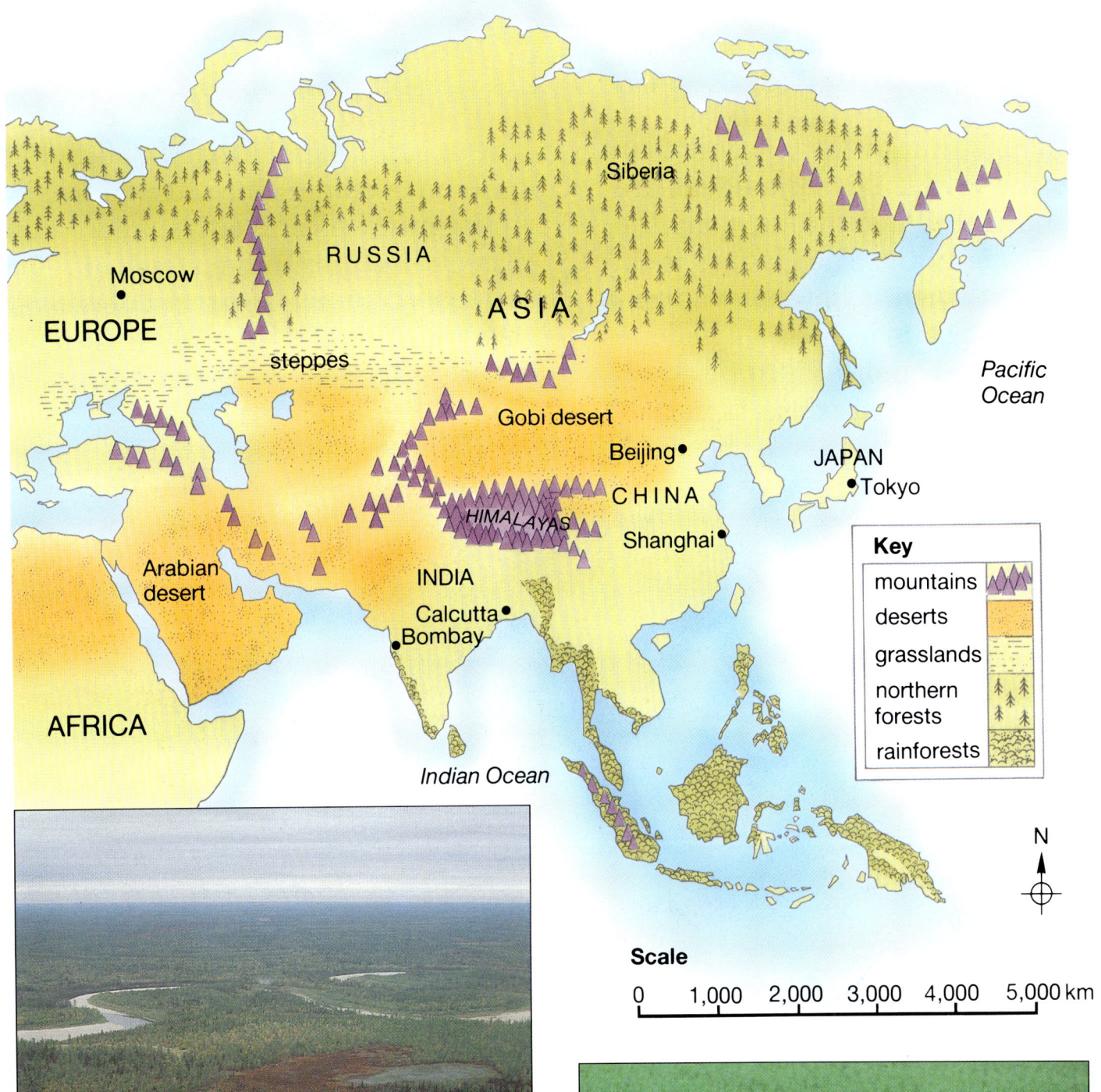

▲ The plains of Siberia are covered with pine trees and swamps.

▲ In South-East Asia people depend on the monsoon rains to make their crops grow well.

Talking and writing

Discuss what you would show on a travel poster of Asia.

57

India - a country in Asia

India is the seventh largest country in the world. The Himalayas are a barrier of mountains along the north of India. The Ganges is the biggest river. It flows down from the mountains, crosses a wide plain, and empties into the Indian Ocean. There are deserts in the west and rocky hills in the south.

India has a population of 850 million people. Some of them live in large towns and cities, and others live in the thousands of villages that are scattered across the countryside. New Delhi is the capital city.

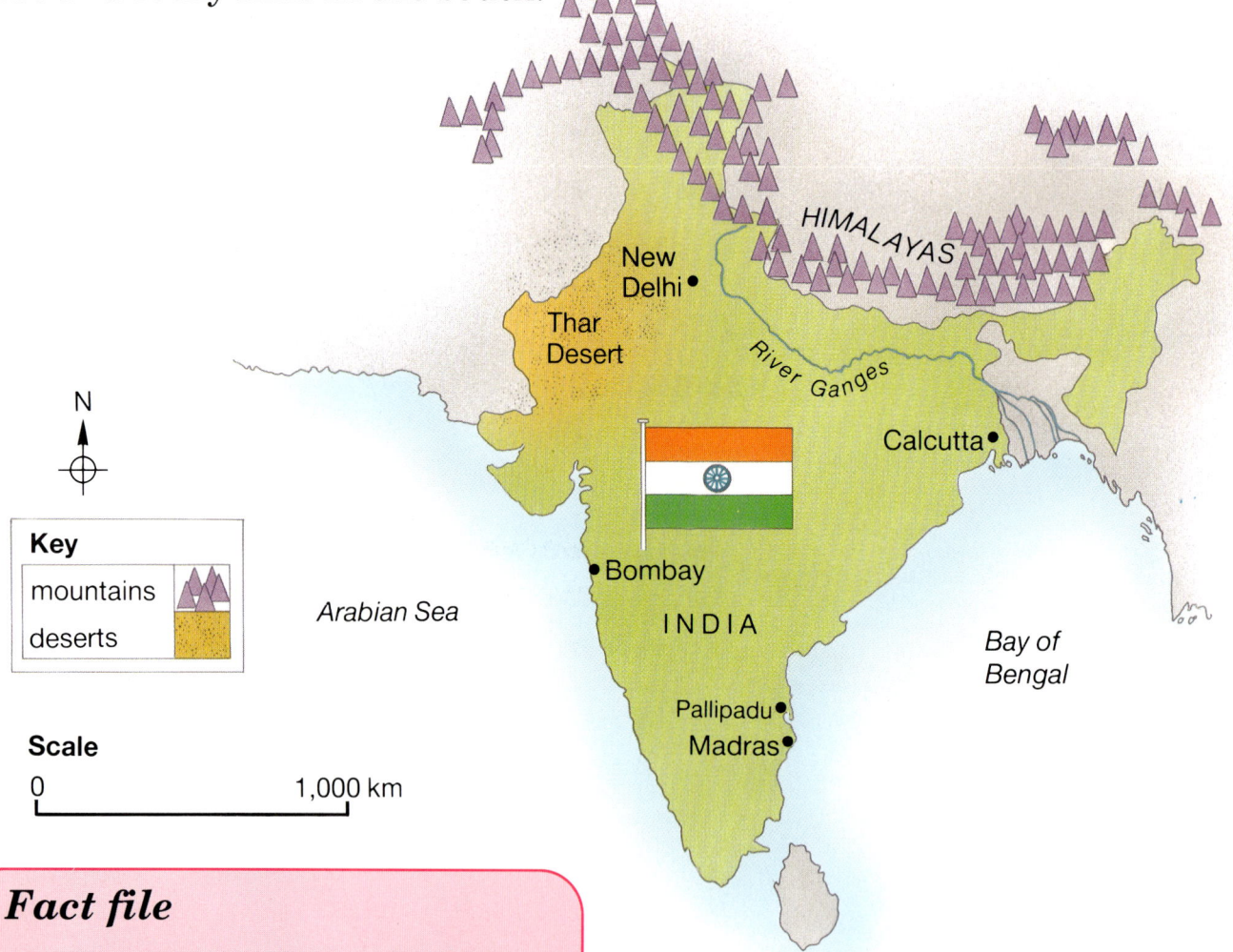

Key
- mountains
- deserts

Scale
0 — 1,000 km

Fact file

- People speak many languages including Hindi and English.
- India has the fourth largest railway network in the world.
- Making clothes is a very important industry.

Things to do

Make a zigzag book about India. It could have a map, photographs and drawings.

Pallipadu - a village in India

My name is Vijaya. I live in a village called Pallipadu in India.

My village is built on the banks of the River Pennar on the east coast of India. There are many old buildings and trees in the village. I think they are very beautiful.

Vijaya

▲ *Farmers use buffaloes to plough the fields.*

There are about 3,000 people in Pallipadu. Most of them are farmers. They grow rice, lentils, peanuts and vegetables. They also keep chickens and buffaloes. The soil is very fertile. This means it is so good that the people can grow two or three crops a year.

Between December and April the weather in Pallipadu is dry and warm. After that it becomes very hot and humid. When the monsoon rains come in July it is cooler.

In November we have very bad storms called cyclones. In 1991 a cyclone caused terrible floods and 130 people were drowned in nearby villages.

Jan	Feb	Mar	Apr	May	Jun	Jul	Aug	Sep	Oct	Nov	Dec
Pleasantly dry and warm			Hot and humid			Monsoon rains			Cyclones		

Clean water is another problem for us. All the water in Pallipadu used to come from wells and hand pumps. A few years ago the government built a water tank. Now there are taps in most of the streets, and we can get water more easily.

Buildings are changing too. In the past, people used to live in houses with thatched roofs and mud walls. Now most of the houses have been rebuilt in brick and cement. This makes the houses stronger and they are not so easily knocked down by cyclones. However, the new houses are small and they get hot inside in summer.

▲ Old and new houses.

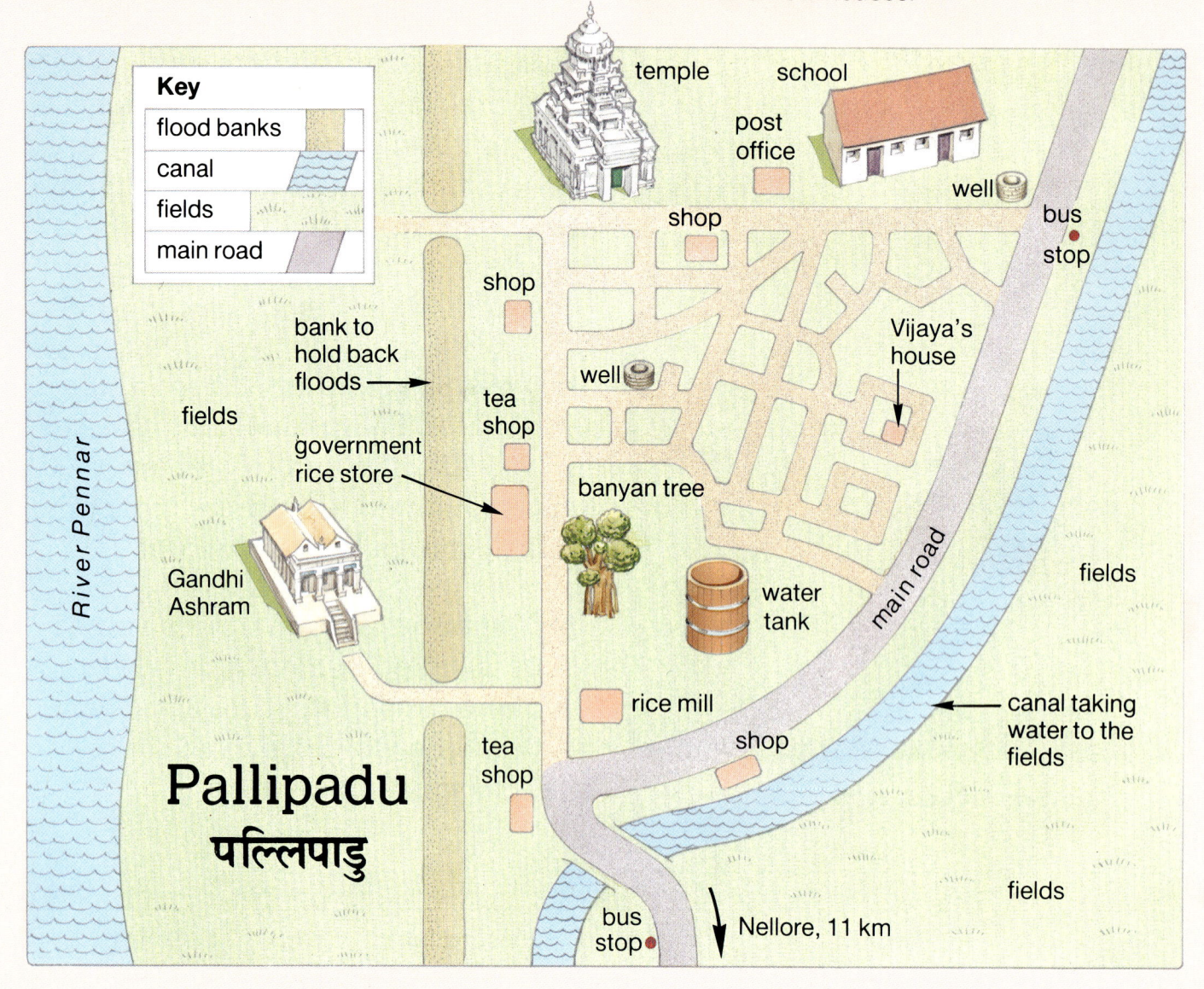

Pallipadu
पल्लिपाडु

Key:
- flood banks
- canal
- fields
- main road

Map labels: River Pennar, temple, school, post office, well, bus stop, shop, Vijaya's house, bank to hold back floods, fields, tea shop, government rice store, well, banyan tree, Gandhi Ashram, water tank, main road, fields, canal taking water to the fields, rice mill, shop, tea shop, bus stop, Nellore, 11 km, fields

60

Nobody in Pallipadu has a car but some people have motor scooters and bicycles. Most of us use the bus which goes to the local town, Nellore. People go there to sell vegetables or to see a film. Often the bus is overcrowded and runs late.

In Pallipadu most people work every day. At different times of the year there are festivals. We go to the temple and afterwards there is dancing and everyone has a holiday.

▲ People enjoy special days like festivals and weddings.

▲ There are many small shops in the town.

Things to do

1. Look at the map of Pallipadu. Make a list of the different buildings in the village. Decide which are the three most important.

2. If Vijaya wrote to your class, what do you think she would say she liked about her life in Pallipadu?

You have learnt

◆ about the landscape of Asia
◆ about different parts of India
◆ about life in an Indian village.

Glossary

British Isles	Britain, Ireland and small islands around their coasts.
cargo	The goods carried in vehicles like ships and planes.
climate	The pattern of weather over many years.
continent	Great blocks of land, such as Africa.
cyclone	A fierce storm which affects parts of Asia.
desert	A dry area where there is very little rain.
environment	The world around us.
equator	An imaginary line around the earth, half-way between the north and south poles.
farm	A place where crops are grown and animals are kept for food.
forestry	Growing trees so they can be sold for money.
geography	The study of the surface of the earth and how people live.
goods	The things which people sell to each other.
habitat	The place where plants and animals live.
hibernate	An animal hibernates when it goes to sleep during the winter months.
landscape	The shape of the land, which can be made up of mountains, hills, valleys and other features.
monsoon rains	Rainy weather which comes after the dry season in South-East Asia.
north pole	The most northerly point on the earth's surface.
oasis	A place in the desert where there is enough water for trees and plants to grow.
ocean	The seas which surround the continents.
planet	A mass of rock and gas which circles around a star or a sun.
plantation	A large farm where only one crop is grown.
plateau	A fairly flat piece of land high up in the mountains.
polar lands	The land and ice around the north and south poles.
pollution	Changes in our surroundings which damage the health of people, plants or animals.
rainforest	Areas of thick forest which are near to the equator.
settlement	The places where people live, such as houses, towns and cities.
south pole	The most southerly point on the earth's surface.
tourist	Someone who visits places on holiday.
transport	The vehicles used by people or goods.
United Kingdom	The country made up of England, Wales, Scotland and Northern Ireland.
water vapour	An invisible gas in the air.

Index

aeroplanes 27, 28, 51
Africa 3, 8, 23, 35
air 2, 8, 13, 40
airports 27, 28, 45
America
　North 3, 26, 34
　South 3, 4, 34
animals 2, 10, 14, 15, 16, 19, 23, 33, 34, 38, 39, 40, 41, 42, 49
Antarctica 3, 14, 40
Asia 3, 4, 23, 34, 56-61
Australasia 3
Australia 34
Austria 23

Bainbridge, Yorkshire 22
Bangladesh 34
birds 10, 42, 49
British Isles 6, 42, 44
Burkina Faso 23
butterflies 39, 42

cattle ranches 34
China 29, 35, 41, 56
climate 14, 22, 35, 51, 56
clouds 8, 9, 13
coast 5
Colombia 40
continents 2, 3, 56
cows 23, 32, 33, 36, 48
crops 16, 17, 32, 33, 34, 36, 52-53, 57, 59

deserts 2, 14, 15, 17, 18, 19, 41, 56, 58
　Gobi 56
　Sahara 14, 17, 23
Edinburgh, Scotland 46-47
England 5, 35, 36
equator 18
Europe 3, 23, 29, 50-55

factories 29
farms 5, 24, 34, 35, 36, 48, 59
　Brimley Farm, Dorset 32-33
fishing 16, 23, 45
food 10, 16, 20, 22, 29, 34, 35, 37, 38, 45, 49, 52
forests 2, 14, 23, 26
France 5, 35, 50-55

game reserves 41
Ghana 35
glaciers 9
goods 26-29, 49
Greenland 16

habitats 38-39, 40, 42, 43, 49
hills 4, 5, 6, 13, 58
houses 17, 22, 23, 24, 60

ice 4, 9, 14, 15, 51
icebergs 9
India 35, 56, 58-61
industries 45, 51, 58
insects 10, 14, 38, 42
Ireland 36
islands 5, 44, 45, 48-49

Kenya 41

lakes 4, 8, 9, 12, 19
landscape 4, 5, 6-7, 12, 22, 36, 44, 51
lorries 26, 29
lowlands 5, 6, 44, 45

maps 6, 12, 18, 30, 36, 40-41, 44, 46, 48, 50, 55, 57, 58, 60
marshes 5, 12
mountains 2, 4, 5, 6, 23, 26, 27, 44, 48
　Alps 23, 50, 51
　Andes 4
　Ben Nevis 45
　Himalayas 4, 56, 58
　Pyrenees 51
Mull, Scotland 48-49
Myanma 23

national parks 40
nature reserves 42
New Zealand 35
north pole 14, 18

oases 17
oceans 2, 8
　Atlantic Ocean 51
　Indian Ocean 58
　Pacific Ocean 2, 5
　Southern Ocean 41
oil 45
orchards 35, 53

Pallipadu, India 59-61
Parnac, Dordogne 52-53
people 5, 10, 20, 26, 27, 28, 40, 41, 56, 58
plantations 35
plants 2, 4, 10, 13, 14, 15, 19, 38, 39, 40, 42, 49
plateaus 4
polar lands 14, 15, 16, 18, 19
pollution 40, 45
ponds 8, 10, 13, 19, 24, 38
puddles 13, 39

railways 29, 45, 51, 58
rain 4, 9, 11, 13, 14, 17, 35, 36, 44, 51, 57
rainforest 14, 18, 56
Renault 54-55
reservoirs 12
rice fields 34
rivers 5, 8, 12, 13, 14, 19, 26, 51
　Ganges 58
　Lot 52
　Seine 51, 54
　Zambezi 8
roads 24, 26, 45
rocks 2, 5, 8, 11
Russia 29, 56

Scotland 36, 44-49
sea 2, 4, 8, 9, 11, 12, 27, 40
settlements 20
sheep 34, 36, 48
ships 27, 29,
shops 24, 37, 49
Siberia, Russia 57
snow 4, 9, 15, 19, 23, 44, 51
soil 4, 5, 8, 10, 11, 13, 36, 39, 52, 59
south pole 18
streams 8, 12, 13
sun 3, 17, 18, 23, 35, 36
swamps 5, 57

tea estates 35
tourism 45, 46, 48, 53
trains 26, 29
transport 26-31, 45, 51, 58
trees 5, 10, 13, 14, 39, 41, 42

United Kingdom 24, 36, 44-49, 50
United States 35, 40

valleys 4, 5
Victoria Falls, Africa 8
villages 17, 20, 22, 23, 24-25, 51, 58,

Wales 5, 36
water 2, 5, 8-13, 15, 17, 22, 26, 27, 41, 60
water vapour 9
weather 4, 14, 15, 16, 19, 36, 44, 51, 59
whales 41
work 16, 23, 28, 32-37, 42, 45, 46, 51, 54-55
Worth, Kent 24-25

63

Published by Collins Educational,
77-85 Fulham Palace Road, London W6 8JB
An imprint of HarperCollins Publishers

© Stephen Scoffham, Colin Bridge, Terry Jewson 1994

First published 1994
Reprinted 1996
98765432

ISBN 0 00 315 470 X

The authors assert the moral right to be identified as the authors of this work.

All rights reserved. No part of this publication may be reproduced, stored in a retrieval system, or transmitted in any form or by any other means, electronic, mechanical, photocopying, recording or otherwise, without the prior permission of the Publisher.

Printed and bound in Italy by Rotolito.

Designed by Chi Leung

Illustrations by Cecilia Fitzsimons pp10, 38-39, 42, 49r; Maltings Partnership pp4-5, 6, 9, 12, 13, 18, 20-22, 24-25, 28, 29, 30, 32-33, 36, 40-41, 44t, 46-47, 48, 50, 53, 55t, 57, 58, 60; Jenny Mumford pp37, 44b, 47c, 49l, 55c, 59; Sally Neave pp34-35, 55b; Lorna Turpin/Linda Rogers Associates p17; Karen Tushingham/Maggie Mundy pp2, 8, 14, 20, 26, 32, 38, 44, 50, 56.

Picture research by Faith Perkins

Photographs reproduced by permission of:
(t=top b=bottom l=left r=right c=centre)
Brian & Cherry Alexander pp9tr & br, 15r; Roy Burton pp48bl, bc & br, 49; J Allan Cash p51br; John Cleare Mountain Camera p48t; COMPIX pp5tr (Mark Both), 8 (David Davis), 59 (A&J Samaya); ECOSCENE p40br (Whittle); Mary Evans Picture Library pp26cr, 27tr & bl; Explorer pp50 (Anne Marie Louvet), 51tl & tr; Richard Goodenough p40tr; Greenpeace p41br (Culley); Robert Harding Picture Library pp4b, 5br, 15l (Jon Gardey), 17 (F Jack Jackson), 23c (Sassoon), 27br (Ian Griffiths), 41tl (Philip Craven); Holt Studios International pp19t & 36tl (Nigel Cattlin), 36bl; Hulton-Deutsch Collection p26tr; Hutchison Photograph Library pp11tr (Liba Taylor), 35b, 57r; The Image Bank p2l (John Wagner Jr); Images of India Picture Agency pp60 & 61t (Roderick Johnson); Terry Jewson pp9tl, 19b, 32, 36tr, 43; Frank Lane Picture Agency p35b (M Clark); John Noble Wilderness Photography pp16r, 35t; Novosti p57l (B Blinchenko); Christine Osborne p34b; David Oswin Photographic Library p16l; PANOS pp11tl (Jeremy Hartley), 23t (Ron Giling), 56bl (Wang Gang Fend), 61b (Jim Holmes); Quadrant Picture Library pp26ct, 26bl, 27tl; Steffan Owen, Quarry Bank School p30bl, cl & cr; Renault UK Ltd p54t; Royal Geographical Society pp9bl (Drew Geldart); 34t (Sitting Images); RSPB pp42ct (M Walter), 42bl, cb & br (C H Gomersall, RSPB & Swift Picture Library p42tr (Dennis Bright); Science Photograph Library p3; Christopher Scoffham 30bl; Stephen Scoffham pp4t, 5tl & bl, 11br, 41tr, 54cl, cr & b, 56t & br; South American Pictures p14 (Tony Morrison); Spectrum pp11bl, 23b; Still Moving Picture Company pp44 (Stephen J Whitehorne), 45l (Douglas Courance); 45r (Wade Cooper), 47 (Paul Tomkins); Still Pictures/Mark Edwards p40c (Paul Harrison); Telegraph Colour Library p2r; Barry Waddams pp7, 31, 52-53, Mike Walter 42tl.

Cover photograph: Durdle Door, Dorset.
Reproduced courtesy of James Davis Travel Photography.